Innovative Community Change Practices

The national recession forced many communities to examine new and innovative ways to promote local economic development, resulting in long-term community changes. New techniques and approaches were used to identify available opportunities and programs which could take advantage of development opportunities. A common theme among the contributions to this book is a focus on building leadership capacity, and several chapters discuss the successful practices which are aimed at bringing new leaders into local development efforts. Especially important are ways to identify youth and young adults, and designing programs that bring them into active leadership roles within community development efforts. On a broader scale, several authors present material regarding building local entrepreneurship capacity, and recognizing that entrepreneurs at different stages in their development have different training and support needs.

The discussions in this book will help local policymakers and development practitioners better understand the various development techniques, and find ways to build capacity within their community, stimulating development. This information will be especially useful for groups interested in engaging youth and populations who, in the past, have not been especially active in discussions about community and economic development.

This book was originally published as a special issue of *Community Development.*

Norman Walzer is Senior Research Scholar at the Center for Governmental Studies, Northern Illinois University, DeKalb, Illinois, USA.

Sam M. Cordes is Director Emeritus at the Center for Regional Development, Purdue University, West Lafayette, Indiana, USA.

Community Development – Current Issues Series
Series Editor: Paul Lachapelle

The Community Development Society (CDS) in conjunction with Routledge/Taylor & Francis is pleased to present this series of volumes on current issues in community development. The series is designed to present books organized around special topics or themes, promoting exploration of timely and relevant issues impacting both community development practice and research. Building on a rich history of over 40 years of publishing the journal, *Community Development*, the series will provide reprints of special issues and collections from the journal. Each volume is updated with the editor's introductory chapter, bringing together current applications around the topical theme.

Founded in 1970, the Community Development Society is a professional association serving both researchers and practitioners. CDS actively promotes the continued advancement of the practice and knowledge base of community development. For additional information about CDS, visit www.comm-dev.org.

You can see further details about this series on the Routledge website on http://www.routledge.com/books/series/CDS/.

Tourism, Planning, and Community Development
Edited by Rhonda G. Phillips

Community Development Approaches to Improving Public Health
Edited by Robert Ogilvie

Community Economic Development
Edited by Rhonda Phillips and Terry L. Besser

Community Leadership Development
Theory, research and application
Edited by Mark A. Brennan

Cooperatives and Community Development
Edited by Rhonda Phillips and Vanna Gonzales

Local Food and Community Development
Edited by Gary Paul Green and Rhonda Phillips

Developing Sustainable Agriculture and Community
Edited by Lionel J. Beaulieu and Jeffrey L. Jordan

Sustainable Rural Development
Sustainable livelihoods and the Community Capitals Framework
Edited by Mary Emery, Isabel Gutierrez-Montes and Edith Fernandez-Baca

Innovative Community Change Practices
Edited by Norman Walzer and Sam Cordes

Community Visioning Programs
Processes and outcomes
Edited by Norman Walzer and Gisele F. Hamm

Innovative Measurement and Evaluation of Community Development Practices
Edited by Norman Walzer, Jane Leonard, and Mary Emery

Innovative Community Change Practices

Edited by
Norman Walzer and Sam M. Cordes

Routledge
Taylor & Francis Group

LONDON AND NEW YORK

First published 2015 by Routledge

2 Park Square, Milton Park, Abingdon, Oxon OX14 4RN
711 Third Avenue, New York, NY 10017, USA

Routledge is an imprint of the Taylor & Francis Group, an informa business

First issued in paperback 2017

British Library Cataloguing in Publication Data
A catalogue record for this book is available from the British Library

ISBN 13: 978-1-138-91343-1 (hbk)
ISBN 13: 978-1-138-08558-9 (pbk)

Typeset in Times New Roman
by RefineCatch Limited, Bungay, Suffolk

Publisher's Note
The publisher accepts responsibility for any inconsistencies that may have
arisen during the conversion of this book from journal articles to book chapters,
namely the possible inclusion of journal terminology.

Disclaimer
Every effort has been made to contact copyright holders for their permission to
reprint material in this book. The publishers would be grateful to hear from any
copyright holder who is not here acknowledged and will undertake to rectify
any errors or omissions in future editions of this book.

Contents

Citation Information

The chapters in this book were originally published in *Community Development*, volume 43, issue 1 (February 2012). When citing this material, please use the original page numbering for each article, as follows:

Chapter 1
Overview of innovative community change programs
Norman Walzer and Sam M. Cordes
Community Development, volume 43, issue 1 (February 2012) pp. 2–11

Chapter 2
InCommons: supporting community-based leadership
Jodi R. Sandfort and Laura Bloomberg
Community Development, volume 43, issue 1 (February 2012) pp. 12–30

Chapter 3
Community leadership development education: promoting civic engagement through human and social capital
Godwin T. Apaliyah, Kenneth E. Martin, Stephen P. Gasteyer, Kari Keating and Kenneth Pigg
Community Development, volume 43, issue 1 (February 2012) pp. 31–48

Chapter 4
Evaluating an asset-based effort to attract and retain young people
William Andresen
Community Development, volume 43, issue 1 (February 2012) pp. 49–62

Chapter 5
Engaging youth in community change: three key implementation principles
David Campbell and Nancy Erbstein
Community Development, volume 43, issue 1 (February 2012) pp. 63–79

Chapter 6
Engaging the underserved in community leadership development: Step Up to Leadership graduates in northwest Missouri tell their stories
Wilson Majee, Scott Long and Deena Smith
Community Development, volume 43, issue 1 (February 2012) pp. 80–94

Chapter 7

Can leadership development act as a rural poverty alleviation strategy?
Ryan Allen and Paul R. Lachapelle
Community Development, volume 43, issue 1 (February 2012) pp. 95–112

Chapter 8

Lessons from the field: mapping Saskatchewan's Pipeline of Entrepreneurs and Enterprises in order to build a provincial operating system for entrepreneurship
Gregg Lichtenstein and Thomas S. Lyons
Community Development, volume 43, issue 1 (February 2012) pp. 113–129

Please direct any queries you may have about the citations to
clsuk.permissions@cengage.com

Notes on Contributors

Ryan Allen is Assistant Professor in the Humphrey School of Public Affairs at the University of Minnesota, Minneapolis, Minnesota, USA.

William Andresen is Associate Professor and Community Resource Development Agent at the University of Wisconsin-Extension, Iron County, Wisconsin, USA.

Godwin T. Apaliyah is a CD Extension Educator in Fayette County, Ohio, USA. He is based in the Rural Sociology Program in the School of Environment and Natural Resources at Ohio State University, Columbus, Ohio, USA.

Laura Bloomberg is Associate Dean of the Humphrey School of Public Affairs at the University of Minnesota, Minneapolis, Minnesota, USA.

David Campbell is a specialist in Co-operative Extension and Director of the California Communities Program at the University of California – Davis, USA.

Sam M. Cordes is Director Emeritus at the Center for Regional Development, Purdue University, West Lafayette, Indiana, USA.

Nancy Erbstein is Assistant Research Professor in the Human Development Graduate Group at the University of California – Davis, USA.

Stephen P. Gasteyer is Associate Professor of Sociology at Michigan State University, East Lansing, Michigan, USA.

Kari Keating is based in the Department of Human and Community Development at the University of Illinois, Urbana-Champaign, Illinois, USA.

Paul R. Lachapelle is an Extension Community Development specialist at Montana State University, Bozeman, Montana, USA.

Gregg Lichtenstein is CEO of Collaborative Strategies, LLC, Margate, New Jersey, USA.

Scott Long is based with the Green Hills Community Action Agency, Trenton, Missouri, USA.

Thomas S. Lyons is Field Family Chair in Entrepreneurship and Professor of Management in the Zicklin School of Business, Baruch College, City University of New York, New York City, USA.

Wilson Majee is Assistant Professor of Health Sciences, and is based in the Community Development Program at the University of Missouri Extension, Princeton, Missouri, USA.

Kenneth E. Martin is Chair of the Department of Extension at Ohio State University, Columbus, Ohio, USA.

Kenneth Pigg is Associate Professor Emeritus in the Department of Rural Sociology at the University of Missouri, Columbia, Missouri, USA.

Jodi R. Sandfort is Associate Professor in the Humphrey School of Public Affairs at the University of Minnesota, Minneapolis, Minnesota, USA.

Deena Smith is based with the Green Hills Community Action Agency, Trenton, Missouri, USA.

Norman Walzer is Senior Research Scholar at the Center for Governmental Studies, Northern Illinois University, DeKalb, Illinois, USA.

Overview of innovative community change programs

Norman Walzer[a] and Sam M. Cordes[b]

[a]Center for Governmental Studies, Northern Illinois University, DeKalb, IL, USA;
[b]Purdue Center for Regional Development, Purdue University, West Lafayette, IN, USA

This Special Issue of the *Journal* is designed to help community development practitioners and scholars in the important roles they play – both directly and indirectly – to foster community betterment. The body of work articulated in this volume builds on a long history of important community development programs and efforts.

Introduction

Communities and neighborhoods, large and small alike, not only have many opportunities but also face challenges and obstacles. How to take advantage of the opportunities and also minimize risks and challenges is paramount to those who live in these neighborhoods and communities. It is the responsibility of community development scholars and practitioners to help inform and support efforts that are most likely to help communities seize opportunities and avoid or minimize the downside. This Special Issue of the *Journal* is designed to help community development practitioners and scholars in the important roles they play – both directly and indirectly – to foster community betterment.

The body of work articulated in this volume builds on a long history of important community development programs and efforts. For example, the economic difficulties in rural areas in the 1980s triggered a round of strategic planning programs designed to evaluate possible development alternatives and plot a course for the future of many small towns. One such initiative was the *Take Charge* program launched in 1990 by the North Central Regional Center for Rural Development (Take Charge) (Ayers et al. 1990). *Take Charge* was adopted and implemented by Cooperative Extension units across the US. The three basic questions raised were: (1) Where have we been? (2) Where do we want to be? (3) How will we get there? An action plan was created during the process with follow-up activities provided by the partners. In addition to providing a solid and well-founded approach to community visioning exercises, the *Take Charge* manual provided materials that can easily be used in working with diverse groups.

The next generation of *Take Charge* was launched in 2001 and was called *Vision to Action* (Green & Borich, 2001). The revisions placed more focus on assets and talents in the community and how they can be mobilized to address high priority problems or issues. The three basic questions of *Vision to Action* are: (1) What do we want to preserve? (2) What do we want to change? (3) What do we want to create? This revised approach also placed greater emphasis on monitoring results and outcomes and the importance of accountability. Such an emphasis is consistent with many initiatives of local and state agencies, the Federal government, foundations and other groups interested in obtaining better estimates of outcomes from investments in local projects.

Many projects and related programmatic efforts spun off from the two generations of *Take Charge*, with a common thread of bringing about positive changes in the communities (Walzer and Hamm, 2012). These diverse approaches are important because they are customized to meet the unique needs of each community. Common among the multitude of programmatic efforts, however, is to build the capacity of community leaders and residents to create, implement and evaluate strategies and tactics that will ultimately raise the quality of life, expand employment opportunities, and/or improve other desired characteristics sought by communities.

Many of the programs and initiatives featured in this volume can trace their roots back to *Take Charge* and/or *Vision to Action*. Such programs and initiatives are needed more than ever due to the current prolonged recession with serious unemployment, outmigration, and related social and political issues.

Another purpose of this Special Issue is to help bring together some of the important but scattered literature about community change, how it can be launched, processes involved, and the outcomes. Such a compilation makes it easier for academics and practitioners to reflect on their own work and improve its effectiveness by considering important factors that have led to the success, and limitations, of the work of others.

Principles of effective practice

In 2010, a team of researchers and practitioners from several Midwestern universities and other organizations[1] received funding from the North Central Regional Center for Rural Development to convene academics and practitioners from long-standing and successful community change programs, mainly from the Midwest, to identify factors that contribute to successful community changes. Participants were selected based on the outcomes that had been obtained from the innovative approaches used in their community change programs, the length of time the programs had been active, and the diversity of populations engaged in the programs. The leaders of these programs met on multiple occasions and, based on their experiences with these and other programs, identified four factors common to successes. These factors are briefly described below and were among the criteria used in selecting the seven articles included in this volume.

Prepare communities for intervention efforts

A consensus exists among program leaders regarding a strong relationship between successful results and time spent preparing participants, regardless of whether it is a far-reaching program or targeted to a specific population or group within the community. Lack of advance preparation or "readiness" in the community may be a significant reason why intervention programs, in some instances, have not obtained desired results.

Three "readiness" factors were identified. First, when the goal is community-wide change, then the entire community must be informed. This is not simply a matter of a widespread awareness of the program and desired outcomes but a willingness to be open to the need for change as well. Part of this participatory education process also involves broad-based involvement, especially by groups and segments of the community population that have not held leadership positions or even participated in similar endeavors. In some instances, programs and initiatives specifically targeted to marginalized groups may be needed before it is possible to realize the full potential of their assets in the broader community change dynamic. Of special importance is encouraging, and then supporting, first time leaders. These leaders face risks in assuming leadership roles; helping them succeed can have lasting effects for the community.

Second, a general awareness and superficial participation in the intervention process is not sufficient; deep and purposeful buy-in is crucial. Because outcomes are likely to take several years to accomplish, local ownership drives successful results. If participants and other residents are not fully committed to the program, they may become distracted by the next of several projects that are launched in the community. All of these factors must be actively considered before a new program or initiative is fully launched.

Third, identifying and strengthening local networks in the community is often key to long-term success and community change. Networks are vital to the successful implementation of the vision, goals, and projects that the intervention process is likely to generate. In many, or even most instances, the networks exist but must be brought to light and activated. These networks can involve business relationships, social groups, and other interactions that can be made even more active and powerful as part of the intervention process. Therefore, it is necessary to identify relevant existing networks in advance and then use their power as part of the intervention process. Often, this will simultaneously lead to the strengthening or broadening of existing networks or in some cases the creation of new networks.

High quality programs

Community development programs and initiatives must be of high quality and address the priority needs, as defined by the community, to hold the attention of participants. It may be tempting to design one program that, with only minor adjustments in delivery, is expected to work in a completely different context or community size. Effective programs and their implementation must recognize the unique local opportunities and capitalize on them to achieve desired outcomes. At least four characteristics of high quality and effective programs were identified by the scholars and practitioners assembled as part of the North Central Regional Development supported project.

First, participants must understand the differences between *program, process*, and *product*. The *program* has a specific purpose and approach intended to accomplish certain outcomes. The program often involves an external partner that is brought into the community in accordance with a prescribed set of events or formats. As noted earlier, it is critical that such a program be sufficiently flexible, adjusting to specific needs in the community.

It is the *process* that ultimately brings about changes within the community and leads to long-term desired outcomes. As it turns out, the process of change can occur through a variety of programs or approaches depending on which is most effective in working with community residents. The process can be difficult to monitor and measure on a regular basis because it depends heavily on the extent and quality of participation by community leaders and residents.

The program typically yields a final *product(s)* which may include a report, community meetings, action plan or other visible measures of outputs that hopefully will lead to a set of desired outcomes in the future. Participants may be tempted to think that the program is over when the product has been delivered. Actually, the product often does no more than sets the stage for subsequent actions – and ongoing *processes* – that will lead to successful outcomes.

Second, it is important that successful outcomes and changes are documented to monitor the need for adjustments in the program, reasons for success and/or to build credibility for the change efforts.

Third, successful programs that accomplish desired results are likely to have solid theoretical underpinnings and incorporate current thinking from the scholarly and professional literature. This approach is important not only to provide the best quality programming but also to gain and/or maintain credibility for the programs.

Finally, when it is possible to link programs or initiatives to major events in the community, it is often easier to build awareness, gain needed support and credibility, and ultimately community ownership. The *Break Through* program pioneered in Arkansas is an excellent example of how community initiatives can be bolstered by helping participants to "think outside the box" and launch challenging new approaches that stretch the current paradigms and set new horizons (Peterson, Levy, & Jones 2012). Programs that set new directions capture the community's attention and can create a major venue around which the community can organize. Several programs featured in this Special Issue have used this type of an approach or strategy.

Effective program implementation

To a large extent this aspect is a dimension of "high quality programs" but justifies additional attention with flexibility and leadership development as key components. As was noted earlier, programs and initiatives must be flexible enough to adjust to local issues that arise, as well as adhere to the program's theoretical underpinnings and mission to maintain credibility. In other words, issues and corrective action must be addressed during programmatic implementation but without violating the basic foundation or parameters of the program or initiative. Otherwise, the entire effort or program can become diverted into a series of short-term issues and distractions.

Building community capacity by encouraging and rewarding risk-takers when they step forward is very important. Leadership development is part of the process and is an important component of the community change and capacity building process. Building the skills of relatively inexperienced local leaders often involves additional programming efforts. In such cases this must be an integral part of the process even when the results or outcomes are not immediately apparent.

A related component of effective programming is to make sure that participants can take actions immediately without feeling a need to "ask permission". This sense of empowerment and accomplishing results require an attitude and approach permitting participants to act confidently. Involving participants in setting goals and expected outcomes from the program can help build buy-in and a greater sense of responsibility for obtaining results. Establishing networks and mobilizing local assets early in the program encourages participants to take action.

Finally, making the community change process an enjoyable and meaningful experience for participants is often essential to success. The approaches used differ across communities and by specific programs. What is common is the need to generate enthusiasm for the program or initiative and pursuit of the outcomes identified. This enthusiasm can be contagious throughout the community, build capacity, and increase the likelihood of achieving the stated goals for change.

Follow-through activities

The fourth major component of successful community change programs is, in many ways, the most important and perhaps the most often overlooked. Community change is a process that residents must pursue and it does not stop with submission of a report or completion of an event. Instead, action is required.

The extent, to which the program or initiative focuses on an action agenda rather than constructing a planning document, makes a substantial difference in terms of achieving and sustaining long-term desirable outcomes. If participants can organize around a set of actions, develop networks that support the effort, and then include a timeline with metrics for completion, they maximize their chances for success and sustainability. The shift in focus on actions and networks is highlighted in the *Strategic Doing* approach advanced by Morrison (2012). In this case, Strategic Action Packs increase the discipline in follow-through efforts in the community by adding structure to the implementation process.

One strategy is to "pick the low hanging fruit" first in order to show what can be accomplished in the program. As participants gain more confidence in what they can do, they will be encouraged to implement even more sophisticated strategies and projects. Extending the confidence to other community leaders and participants is an important outcome of the change process.

A related strategy is to focus on future opportunities for the community instead of working to correct past problems. While past events may limit future options, change programs are more likely to succeed when they build on community assets or strengths rather than only on finding remedies for perceived or real problems in the community.

The diversity in age and socioeconomic status of community residents means that multiple communication approaches must be used throughout the process, including in the initial stage of follow-through activities. For example, younger residents are more likely to rely on social networking techniques while older residents may obtain more information from traditional news media sources. Building networks using different, but complimentary, approaches is an important element in maintaining the momentum of community change.

Another element of effective follow-through is to celebrate and publicize successes. Doing so encourages participants to stretch even more, helps community residents understand what has occurred, likely brings additional participants to the table and builds credibility for the efforts underway. As noted previously, communicating these successes throughout the community will involve a variety of tools and media to reach all population segments.

Maintaining a persistent approach to follow-up is absolutely essential to successful community change processes. Effective follow-through requires strong networks of interested participants committed to positive outcomes from the change process. Some programs include community coaches who work with participants and local groups to keep them on track and help explore new opportunities. Participants must receive regular encouragement and feel that they have succeeded in the community-wide effort. Having broad community-wide goals that residents can embrace facilitates building a support base to maintain a persistent follow-up. One option or response to the notion of "persistence" is to be more explicit and deliberate about the importance of sustainability and resiliency. An active support base recognizing that "change is inevitable but progress is optional" is what will bring successful community change on a recurring basis.

Overview of chapters

The programs, initiatives and projects described in subsequent articles, in one way or another, have succeeded in accomplishing community change objectives using a variety of innovative approaches. They also match up well with the four factors or principles of effective practice and programming described in the previous section.

While several articles focus, in one way or another on building leadership capacity, they illustrate the diverse approaches that can be used in meeting program objectives. A common theme running through several articles includes the importance of building leadership capacity among youth and/or other groups who are not usually part of the traditional leadership structure in communities. Because communities have different leadership programs underway, with widely differing formats and delivery systems, it is important to share resources and provide a setting in which a systems approach is available.

Several foundations in Minnesota created an *InCommons* arrangement to provide such an environment and Sandfort and Bloomberg describe the results of that approach. Although the early work is promising, long-term outcomes cannot be tracked or predicted because this initiative is in the awareness building and developmental stage. It is included in this volume partly because it is a robust example of the role that interacting "virtually" and the Web can play in sharing knowledge and techniques among a broad base of stakeholders. The "open-source" nature of *InCommons* and the democratization of knowledge and information via the web-based platform mean successes in one community can be shared quickly with others in the network. Of special importance is the ability to communicate with not only members of the group but also to access available expertise anywhere.

The extensive communications and networking ability available through large scale programs such as *InCommons* also build leadership capacity by encouraging other communities to launch similar initiatives. The networking among participating communities means that leadership can be developed and promoted at a broad geographic level, such as an entire state as is the case with *InCommons*.

Apaliyah, Martin, Gasteyer, Keating, and Pigg (2012) in a study of community leadership development education programs (CLDE), report the successes of a broad range of leadership programs in preparing residents to participate more effectively in community decisions. In doing so, participants build their own human capital and then use it to build and strengthen both bonding social capital and bridging social capital. The stronger connections within the community allow CLDE participants to assume greater leadership roles and make stronger contributions to the overall community development activities underway. Using the Community Capitals (Emery et al. 2006) framework, Apaliyah et al. conclude that community-level financial and political capital are also generated by CLDE participants.

The research design of the Apaliyah et al. (2012) study is also worthy of note. First, an experimental design is used, something that is uncommon in evaluating community development programs, including leadership programs. Specifically, the authors create "control groups" to use as a comparison base for what is happening with those who are participating in the various leadership development programs being studied. In addition, another aspect of the design enables the researchers to ascertain the extent to which benefits to the individual participants are also translated or manifested into greater civic engagement and community betterment.

The research builds on several other components of successful intervention programs including preparing a community for community change. The CLDE program builds a stronger cohesion within the community and enhances the leadership capacity. Communities with a higher number of CLDE programs are better positioned to understand issues facing the community and have a better grasp of what remedies might succeed. They know the assets and how the important players might come together to implement successful programs. CLDE participants are also positioned to provide continuous follow-through on the action plan created during the intervention program.

For many rural communities, the loss of youth and the potential "brain drain" continues to be an obstacle to long-term community growth and development. Andresen reports on attempts in northern Wisconsin and the western portion of the Upper Peninsula in Michigan (Goebic Range) to retain and attract young people to stabilize populations and build a competitive workforce. The region has a history of population declines with the "brain drain" so familiar to many rural areas that can ultimately lead to stagnation and higher poverty rates.

The project surveyed high school students, community college freshmen and young adults to identify the importance of area characteristics in decisions about where to live. They also asked recent in-migrants to the area about how they perceived the region *vis-à-vis* the various characteristics that may influence location decisions. Local development practitioners then focused on those factors that were viewed positively and were also important in the location decision. Efforts were then put in place to strengthen this set of assets, to promote them, and to connect high school and college students to these assets. An associated set of outcomes – short-term, mid-term, and long-term – were also delineated to provide an overall evaluation framework for this ambitious initiative.

The Wisconsin–Michigan project incorporated several components of successful community change discussed earlier. First, the program builds on community strengths using a solid data base of information about the region. Second, the program targets a population segment, specifically young adults, seen as key to regional stability in the future in terms of community capacity and leadership. Third, the program mobilizes community assets, builds on past successes, and incorporates a new approach with high expectations. Fourth, the program focuses on the future, rather than the past, in pursuing long-term sustainability for the region. Finally, the program has a cohesive and comprehensive evaluation design to provide ongoing feedback and the basis for mid-course adjustments over a 10-year planning horizon.

Many communities have programs designed to improve the skills and development of youth and some have broad-based community betterment projects and initiatives. Rarely, however, are these two programmatic domains integrated in a purposeful fashion. The work of Campbell and Erbstein (2012) is a refreshing example of what can happen and what can be learned when these two foci are brought together. Such an approach was taken in seven communities in Sacramento, California.

For many, this approach represents new territory with high risks and the implementation of such an effort can be challenging. Hence, the program must build in safeguards. The specific scope or target of the community development initiatives did not seem to be as important as other considerations in leading to successful outcomes. For example, successful projects included engagement by adults who recognize the potential of youth. Providing support for youth as they assumed leadership roles within the community was also a critical consideration. This often required a reorientation of projects. Through these experiences, the capacity and interests of youth were built as they participated in community development efforts. The outcomes led to students who are better integrated into the community. In some instances, their families benefitted from the experiences as well. Likewise, the adult participants gained new respect for the potential of including youth and the contributions they can make to local development.

Effective community change intervention requires broad-based support. Campbell and Erbstein focus on the importance of bringing youth and young adults into the community change process. An equally important population is low income residents. Wilson, Long, and Smith (2012) focus on the latter population and report on a transformational program called step up to leadership (SUL) in the state of Missouri. The program uses many of the building blocks cited by other authors but focuses more on disadvantaged residents, especially women, in an effort to better integrate them into community enhancement efforts.

Interviews with SUL graduates and other participants were part of the data collection and evaluative process. Results suggest that SUL participants improved their ability to interact with others; gained increased understanding of civic responsibility and awareness of local resources; improved their knowledge of and engagement in community issues; and grew in self-confidence, employability and optimism. The hope is that these program participants can also play an inspirational role for peers, create strong bonding social capital among participants, and generate productive bridging social capital between the participants and influential people in the community. Ultimately, this leads to better opportunities for low income populations and a strengthened overall community dynamic.

Allen and Lachapelle (2012) report on the skills and roles played by community coaches in community development initiatives. Their reference point is *Horizons*, a relational leadership development program that has reached nearly 300 communities in seven states. Its goal is to reduce poverty in rural areas by promoting local leadership and focusing community action on poverty reduction strategies. The educational and leadership components focus on the causes of poverty, consequences, and how collective action within the community could bring about change through effective leadership. Despite a common curriculum, the experiences of *Horizons* communities have varied tremendously. Allen and Lachapelle (2012) argue that much of this variation may be due to different implementation strategies and tactics and that the "community coach" variable may be of special importance.

In order to explore this concept further, their study examines the *Horizons* programs in Montana and Minnesota. Each state used a different type of community coach. In Montana a local Extension Educator from within the community was used. In Minnesota the coach did not live in the community but was hired with significant expertise in leadership and community knowledge although relatively little local knowledge of the community's history and institutional infrastructure.

Results of the study suggest that *Horizons* has the potential to profoundly affect a community's sense of identity and fundamentally change residents' willingness to become engaged in their communities to make improvements. In terms of the skills and roles of the community coaches, the authors argue for a balance between content expertise and community connectedness. Too much of one of these qualities in a coach without enough of the other may reduce the potential of a program to change communities. This principle likely holds for a broad variety of community change initiatives.

While many authors focused on leadership development within a community, the work of Lichenstein and Lyons (2012) is much different by concentrating on a systems-wide approach to entrepreneurship development for the province of Saskatchewan. Although system-oriented and province-wide, flexibility is emphasized with special importance placed on recognizing the very different skills, needs and backgrounds of entrepreneurs. The Lichenstein and Lyons' system framework recognizes both the skills of entrepreneurs and the stage or life-cycle of the business. These two dimensions are the foundation for creating the Saskatchewan Pipeline of Entrepreneurs and Enterprises.

Planning and implementation of the framework involved a broad scope of awareness building and data gathering activities, including presentations and interviews with entrepreneurs and service providers. In addition to mapping a pipeline for the entire province, 18 other pipelines were identified and mapped: 13 regional areas; three demographic groups; and two market sectors. The pipeline framework proved useful in generating a variety of important programmatic activities, meaningful recommendations and other actionable items and outcomes.

Although much of the emphasis was at the provincial level, key community development principles were employed, such as inclusivity and modeling other "best practices" of the change process as the Pipeline was designed and made operational. Results to date include (a) an increase in cooperation among service providers; (b) a new way of thinking about entrepreneurship; (c) a customer-centered, rather than too-centered, approach by service providers; and (d) a greater appreciation for systems thinking.

Summary

Community change is difficult in most communities but, as subsequent articles show, effective programs can bring about change. Several key considerations for success were identified earlier in this overview article and subsequent authors will describe programs that have used these principles to cause effective changes in their communities.

Key among the common characteristics of these programs is the concept of community readiness and the importance of strong local champions and leaders. Sensitivity to the specific needs and contributions that can be made by youth, low-income populations and women are also critical elements of the community change process. In addition, community change is both about the science and the art. For example, successful programs tend to be built on solid theoretical and research foundations. However, strong program design is a necessary, but not sufficient condition, "for success". Due diligence, creativity, and flexibility in the implementation phase become the sufficient conditions.

Another common characteristic of the exemplary programs and initiatives featured in this volume is the capacity to think both short-term and long-term, and build a strong evaluation component along this time horizon.

Finally, successful programs must build the capacity for the change process to continue and to create a comfort level with change and the importance of community resiliency to address unforeseen challenges and opportunities.

We noted earlier that "change is inevitable, but progress is optional." Community development scholars and practitioners have the important role and responsibility of helping communities see progress, not just change, as something that is inevitable. The articles in this Special Issue hopefully will contribute to that outcome.

Note

1. This group includes representatives from Iowa State University, Michigan State University, Northern Illinois University, Purdue University and the Heartland Center for Leadership.

References

Allen, R., & Lachapelle, P.R. (2012). Can leadership development act as a rural poverty alleviation strategy? *Community Development – Special Issue, 43*(1), xx–xx.

Apaliyah, G.T., Martin, K.E., Gasteyer, S.P., Keating, K., & Pigg, K. (2012). Community leadership development education: Promoting civic engagement through human and social capital. *Community Development – Special Issue, 43*(1), xx–xx.

Ayres, J., Cole, R., Hein, C., Huntington, S., Kobberdahl, W., Leonard, W., & Zetocha, D. (1990). *Take charge: Economic development in small communities.* Ames, IA: North Central Regional Center for Rural Development.

Campbell, D., & Erbstein, N. (2012). Engaging youth in community change: Three key implementation principles. *Community Development – Special Issue, 43*(1), xx–xx.

Emery, M., Fey, S., & Flora, C. (2006). Using community capitals to develop assets for positive community change. *CD Practice.* Retrieved from http://www.comm-dev.org/index.php?option=com_content&view=article&id = 70%20itemid=81

Green, G., & Borich, T. (2001). *Vision to action: Take charge too.* Ames, IA: North Central Regional Center for Rural Development.

Lichenstein, G., & Lyons, T. (2012). Lessons from the field: Mapping Saskatchewan's Pipeline of Entrepreneurs and Enterprises in order to build a provincial operating system for entrepreneurship. *Community Development – Special Issue, 43*(1), xx–xx.

Morrison, E. (2012). Strategic Doing for Community Development. In N. Walzer & G.F. Hamm (Eds.), *Community visioning programs* (Chapter 9, pp. 156–177). London and New York: Routledge Taylor and Francis Group.

Peterson, M., Levy, E., & Jones, J. (2012). Breakthrough solutions: A new paradigm for strategic visioning. In N. Walzer & G.F. Hamm (Eds.), *Community visioning programs* (Chapter 10, pp. 178–196). London and New York: Routledge Taylor and Francis Group.

Walzer, N., & Hamm G.F. (2012). *Community visioning programs.* London and New York: Routledge Taylor and Francis Group.

Wilson, M., Long, S., & Smith, D. (2012). Engaging the underserved in community leadership development: Step Up to Leadership graduates in northwest Missouri tell their stories. *Community Development – Special Issue, 43*(1), xx–xx.

InCommons: supporting community-based leadership

Jodi R. Sandfort and Laura Bloomberg

Humphrey School of Public Affairs, University of Minnesota, USA

Cohort-based community leadership programs (CLPs) are a common approach to enhancing knowledge, skills, and networks within a particular community. However, the CLP model is resource intensive and, as a result, limited in impact. This article describes an alternative approach being undertaken on a statewide scale. InCommons is focused on activating a network that lets people find each other so they can share credible knowledge, resources, and insights for solving community problems. One dimension involves finding and sharing the information people need in a leadership commons. Another offers support through well-facilitated gatherings that allow communities to make progress in spite of thorny differences. Using a participatory action research (PAR) approach, we explain the theory of action informing the whole initiative and assess initial implementation in terms defined by community leaders. As such, this article provides practical insights for those interested in increasing the scale and impact of their work with community-based leaders.

Introduction

The 2009 Nobel Prize for Economics was awarded to political scientist Elinor Ostrom for her work on a new model of collective action she calls the Commons. Within western capitalist democracies economists have posited that self-interest creates a "tragedy of the commons" because individuals deplete shared resources for private gain (Hardin, 1968). In contrast, Ostrom and her colleagues draw attention to situations, where communities leverage trust and cooperation to develop and share "common-pool resources," observing that, sometimes, traditional divisions between public and private are inaccurate (Bollier, 2007; Lessig, 2001). Among other things, Ostrom and colleagues examine how *research-based knowledge* can be shared as a common resource (Hess & Ostrom, 2007); informed by Ostrom's model, this article highlights a statewide initiative focused on sharing the *practical knowledge* of community-based leaders.

In late 2010, following 18 months of planning and design work, an array of institutional partners – including regional foundations, Minnesota's land grant university, statewide media, religious, and cultural institutions – launched

InCommons. The initiative focuses on encouraging and supporting the courageous leadership necessary to engage communities and solve problems. Yet, like a few recent efforts (Wituk, Ealey, Clark, Heiny, & Meissen, 2005), InCommons focuses on nurturing community leadership at a statewide scale. To achieve this reach, each institutional partner commit sits own staff resources to help develop anew "town square" for community-based leaders (Public Strategies Group, 2009). Explicitly, InCommons focuses on supporting leadership acts (Daloz, Keen, Keen, & Parks, 1996; Earl, 2007; Parks, 2005; Pigg, 1999; Senge, Scharmer, Jaworski, & Flowers, 2004), rather than working exclusively with individuals holding positions of formal authority. InCommons also highlights the need for leadership in places where contrary world views and knowledge collide, where attention to the common good is needed (Block, 2009; Crosby & Bryson, 2005). In it, we conceptualize "community" broadly, as a group of individuals who share something significant – geography, religion, age, or ethnicity.

This article describes a participatory action research (PAR) approach woven into the initiative's core. We describe the initial research grounding the project and our resulting theory of action that shaped the strategies and tactics employed. We also assess the implementation of InCommons to date, in relation to both community leaders' criteria of success and concepts from our theory of action. This approach, and the newness of the initiative, does not allow an assessment of long-term outcomes, per se. Rather by describing and assessing the emergence of this ambitious initiative, the hope is to motivate others to consider how community-based leadership might be supported on a larger scale.

Research approach and data sources

In the InCommons initiative, we adopted an explicit PAR approach. McIntyre (2008) describes PAR as a "braided process of exploration, reflection, and action" focused on articulating and exploring a theory of action, examining impact, and providing relevant information that enables stakeholders to make programmatic adjustments quickly. While, in practice, PAR takes many forms, it is typically based on five key tenets. First, the research process and assessment are contextual; their relevance is determined by local stakeholders and the degree to which research provides insight into practice. Second, the evaluative criteria of assessment are determined by participants as they act and learn over time, rather than a priori by formal theory. Third, the PAR process is best understood as development evaluation (Patton, 2007) not process or summative evaluation. Rather than making definitive judgments of success or failure, its active purpose is to name problems, propose solutions, and use data to engage in continuous improvement in an initiative. Fourth, as a research approach, PAR places a premium on stakeholder engagement, seeking to include multiple voices, thereby enhancing awareness, and empowerment in the process. Finally, the active interplay of research and practice promotes learning among participants and researchers alike.

The PAR applied to InCommons produces evidence about the ongoing process of change and can be shared with a broad audience to promote formative learning among the key stakeholders closest to the work (McTaggart, 1997; Patton, 2002). Given the initiative's ambition – and the authors' dual roles as active participants and researchers – this approach was the most prudent to employ in this case.

Our analysis and resulting theory of action benefit from an array of data sources, summarized in Table 1. First, we draw upon a phone survey of 400 randomly-sampled households conducted in Fall, 2009 is part of the assessment of community need (Wilder, 2009). Survey participants, ranging in age from 18 to 95, were asked a

Table 1. Data sources informing emergent theory of action and early implementation of InCommons.

Data source	Key questions addressed	Informants	Analysis
Phone survey: Wilder Research (2009)	• What are the most significant state and community problems? • What is the nature of this community and our leaders? • What is our assessment of our quality of life?	Four hundred randomly-sampled individuals	Quantitative descriptive summary of responses to forced choice questions
Structured community meetings: Rausch and MartinRogers (2010)	• What are the most significant state and community problems? • What is the nature of this community and our leaders? • What is our assessment of our quality of life?	Seven hundred and ninety-seven representatives of culturally specific groups under-represented in the phone survey (e.g. African American, Native American, Hmong, Latino, Liberian, and Somali)	Quantitative descriptive summary of responses to forced choice questions
Interviews with formal leaders: Grassroots Solutions (2010)	• What does it mean to engage communities to solve problems? • How does one support community engagement efforts? • How does one connect and engage individuals and civic institutions with the tools and spaces that could be created through an initiative like InCommons?	Forty representatives from civic institutions, networking organizations, advocacy groups, leadership programs, and the media	Qualitative analysis of key emergent themes
Interviews with non-positional community leaders: Brown et al. (2010)	• Why do individuals choose to exercise leadership? • How do leaders engage other individuals and their communities? • What do leaders need do to sustain and/or grow community engagement?	Twenty-five individuals without formal authority but recognized as community leaders, sampled to represent gender, age, and geography	Qualitative analysis of key emergent themes

series of questions to identify the most significant state and community problems and community assets, assess their quality of life and community leadership. The responses were weighted based on 2008 American Community Survey to guarantee gender and age representation. To ascertain how these issues were experienced by ethnic groups under-represented in the statewide picture, the researchers held eight community meetings focused on the same questions. The meetings were hosted by community organizations and religious communities who recruited 797 participants from the African American, Latino, Hmong, Somali, Liberian, and Native American communities (Rausch & MartinRogers, 2010).

We also draw on data from 40 semi-structured interviews conducted with representatives from Minnesota civic institutions, advocacy groups, leadership programs, and the media. Semi-structured telephone interviews were conducted by consultants as part of a preliminary engagement audit (Grassroots Solutions, 2010). The interviews elicited these formal leaders' insights about engaging others in public problem solving and their opinions about essential supports for community leadership. All interviews were transcribed, coded inductively, and deductively using QSR NVivo 8 software (Lewins & Silver, 2007) and summarized in developmental reports to the InCommons partnership team.

Our own University research team conducted 25 additional semi-structured interviews with non-positional and community-based leaders (Brown, Fleetham, Shurilla, & Simonson, 2010). The sample was developed through a snow-ball technique focused on identifying individuals from diverse backgrounds who were recognized community leaders. Participants ranged in age from 24 to 78, with representatives from ethnic minority groups included. The participants were asked questions about community involvement and leadership, engagement tools, and essential resources. All interviews were transcribed, coded inductively, and deductively using QSR NVivo 8 software and summarized in developmental reports.

Finally, we reviewed and analyzed significant initiative documents, including engagement, communications, and business plans were conducted. Throughout, we compiled materials and reviewed notes from stakeholder meetings, working groups, and events. As part of the initiative PAR process, these materials are assessed in relation to emerging theories of action and actual initiative implementation.

Determining and responding to community needs

Our multi-faceted analysis clearly indicated that, like many Americans at the beginning of the twenty-first century, people in Minnesota are concerned about the seeming proliferation of social, economic, and environmental problems and the apparent inability of traditional institutions to respond to them.

While local problems are quite tangible, the broad community phone survey documented that solutions are often illusive. The poor economy, K–12 education, and healthcare were the most frequently cited problems. Only 38% of respondents thought people in their community understood community problems; and only 40% reported their community was effective at solving problems and improving the quality of life. Reported levels of trust of among formal leaders – business, elected officials, and cultural elites – were also low and averaging 63%. However, 90% of respondents were hopeful and optimistic about the future. Three-quarters reported a sense of urgency to solve their community's biggest problems and 75% also reported that they believed people like them could have at least a moderate impact in making their community a better place to live.

Data from under-represented ethnic groups were similar, yet brought different issues into focus. While participants also were concerned with the economy, education, and healthcare, they were significantly less likely to see their community as effective in solving problems and improving their quality of life. Participants were less willing to define communities geographically, rather they focused on ethnic or cultural affinity. Taken together, these data informed the emerging theory of action; while problems certainly exist, the community would improve by moving from a focus on problems to one stressing possibilities, generosity, and restoration. We needed to broaden our lens beyond a focus on geographic communities to recognize the importance of communities of affiliation.

Analysis of semi-structured interviews with formal and informal, non-positional leaders revealed a belief that community-level change requires both leadership and an engaged community (or "organized base") to move an idea or solution forward. Those interviewed reflected that people exercise leadership because of passion, self-interest, and invitations from others who recognize their potential. They act in ways that show they can listen well, bring a variety of perspectives to the table, and share power and responsibilities with others. Leadership and engagement of others do not just happen; it requires a vehicle (a need or topic), face-to-face relationship building, and a long-term commitment.

Our interview analysis also pointed to the importance of particular resources for engaging others. Participants reported a need to access others' stories of success and failure, tap into relevant information filtered by credible entities, and connect in meaningful ways with others engaged in community-level change. To sustain their efforts or have larger impact, participants emphasized the importance of developing new relationships, accessing tools, and having opportunities to learn with others how to build new skills. When asked how InCommons needed to evolve, participants stressed that while scale was important, the initiative also must be grounded in real community presence and promoted over time. InCommons should involve people who are credible because they have performed community-level work. Finally, the initiative should evolve through shared ownership with community leaders, even as it is supported by staff within the institutional partner organizations.

These diverse data sources and ongoing analysis of their meaning directly shaped InCommons' theory of action and initial implementation.

InCommons theory of action

Rather than using one social science theory or framework, the program theory of action draws on an array of concepts to help develop a plausible and sensible model of how InCommons might work (Bickman, 1987). Weiss (1995, p. 72) suggests such theories help "represent the stories that people tell about how problems arise and how they can be solved ... These stories ... whether they are true or false, are potent forces." In this case, the theory is that a statewide network can support and amplify the courage and skills of community-based leadership. While activities in the network will be decentralized, and emerge in relation to community concerns, the network itself is bolstered by several essential propositions.

Proposition #1: Funders can positively impact systems change by relinquishing some decision-making control.

Scholars have long debated whether or not private foundations realize their potential in making social change (Bailin, 2004; Heifetz, Kania, & Kramer, 2004; McKersie, 1999). Philanthropy is a unique institution, insulated from both the political accountability of government and the market demands of business. Because private foundations possess this freedom and significant financial resources, their potential for impact is high. However, often widely heralded initiatives fail to achieve their promised objectives. Some private foundations now employ a range of strategies and use diverse tools to shore up their operations and improve effectiveness (Fulton & Blau, 2005; Sandfort, 2008; Silver, 2004).

When developing these strategies, funders must first grapple with their values and goals to identify a unique focus (Frumkin, 2006). They also must consider a thorny two-fold question: *How do we instigate change* and *How do we sustain it?* McDonnell and Elmore (1987) suggest a continuum of such strategies that – when applied to philanthropic activities – highlights multiple paths to increasing effectiveness. One strategy involves imposing mandates that establish specific rules intended to govern designated actions and ensure compliance. While compliance with mandates often follows, it is difficult to sustain compliance after the grant funding ends. Another strategy of inducement is more commonly used by foundations because it involves using their key resource – money – to inspire specific actions, such as replications of a model programs deemed successful elsewhere. However, research increasingly documents that replicated models often are less successful than the original intervention (Gira, Kessler, & Poertner, 2004). A third philanthropic strategy is capacity building, which is less prescriptive than mandates or inducements but entails investing in material or human resources to insure progress toward or achievement of desired results.

A final strategy for resolving these questions is to focus on system change. This approach shifts authority among sectors and requires private funders to divest themselves of authority to mandate, induce specific activity, or define specific narrow results. Instead, funders embrace the ambiguity within complex systems for the potential of more significant, long-term results aligned with a community's self-identified needs. Normatively, none of these four change strategies is inherently more desirable than any other; ideally, a private foundation establishes the optimal fit between their goals, desired outcome, and any of these approaches.

The goal of InCommons focuses on inspiring and supporting the courageous leadership necessary to engage communities and make progress on thorny challenges. As such, a strategy of mandates or inducements would not be effective. While many community leadership initiatives focus on capacity building, the foundations involved in InCommons were more ambitious. They embarked on a systems change strategy, where they released control and engaged others in developing ways to achieve the goal.

The initial ideas emerged from a design lab sponsored by one of the foundations and a state land-grant university, aligned in their desires to better support and magnify the work of community leaders (Aman, 2011; Public Strategies Group, 2009). The designers envisioned a new civic infrastructure, where leaders could find and share both practical knowledge gleaned from experience, and resources, such as research and tools, developed in other ways. Implementing this vision required finding other large institutional partners willing to change their operations and demonstrably support systems change.

Initially, six other statewide institutions agreed and – without large financial grants from the foundations – dedicated senior manager and staff time to co-create the initial parameters. Together, organizers began to imagine a network supporting dialog about collective challenges, exchanging problem-solving resources, and showcasing leaders engaging others to move issues forward. The communities – rather than the foundations or institutional partners – determine the substantive issues being highlighted (Pigg, 1999). This approach required institutional partners themselves to experiment with new practices for working with communities.

Proposition #2: Sharing practical knowledge as commons resources can enable community-based leadership.

Another dimension of the InCommons theory of action is grounded in supporting the development and sharing of a common pool of practical knowledge. Traditionally, leadership scholars studied individuals, trying to ascertain the traits, behaviors, and skills which enabled them to mobilize followers (Burns, 2003; Cohen & March, 1974; Thomas, 1988). Many scholars now focus on leadership activities, recognizing that most individuals can act in ways that inspire others and create change in a specific setting (Crosby & Bryson, 2005; Earl, 2007; Kouzes & Posner, 2007; Nohria & Khruana, 2010). Making this conceptual shift, community-based leadership can be seen as a unique phenomenon, based on the specific community's knowledge, skills, and sources of authority that confer power (Pigg, 1999).

For people interested in community development, strengthening and enhancing this type of leadership can be a potent strategy (Emery, Fernandez, Gutierrez-Montes, & Butler Flora, 2007; Pigg, 1999). Formal community leadership programs (CLPs) can develop from this orientation and provide opportunities for participants to learn community-specific information, co-create common purpose, and develop new networks of influence. Often these programs operate by bringing diverse people together in a cohort over time to enable deeper learning. While scholars have studied the success of CLPs in meeting these goals, the generalizability of such examinations are usually limited to a small scale and the mechanisms of actual influence remain challenging to ascertain (Brown & Nylander, 1998; Wituk et al., 2005). However, it does seem that community characteristics and training practices can create social capital, build trust, bridge differences, and engage others (Chazdon & Lott, 2010; Mandell, 2010).

Rather than sponsoring cohort-based CLPs, the InCommons theory of action emphasizes these expectations of reciprocity and trust to engage more people as leaders. This initiative creates a leadership commons to generate and share the resources people need to take leadership roles in communities. At its most basic, *commons* is a way of referring to resources shared by a group, the things it inherits, creates, and monitors jointly. Such things are not held by the enclosures of financial markets or governments but are rather understood to be free, with open access. Traditionally, public service activity, such as volunteerism, and institutions that provide open access to resources, such as libraries, played important roles supporting the commons (Boyte, 2004; Daloz et al., 1996; Lohmann, 1992). Yet, social activists and scholars are beginning to reassert the importance of commons-based solutions to broader social, environmental, and economic problems given growing concerns about the undue influence of the market on civic life (Bollier, 2007, 2008; Boyte, 2011; Poteete, Janssen, & Ostrom, 2010).

Scholars studying shared natural resource systems – fisheries, forests, land, and water – find many examples, where individual interests are met by attending to collective needs (Dietz, Ostrom, & Stern, 2003; Lam & Ostrom, 2010; Ostrom, 1990, 2010). Sharing does not deplete resources, if they are adequately protected. But the nature of the protection must be created by the people using the resources. They must commit to providing, managing, and governing them to assure sustainability of resources for all.

Information communication technologies create new opportunities. The interactive internet enables sharing creative and knowledge products, such as photographs, music, and scientific research, with significantly reduced transaction costs. The advent and rapid development of Wikipedia – whose content is donated and monitored by volunteer contributors around the globe – is one often cited example (Bollier, 2008; Tapscott & Williams, 2006). Many other shared resources now exist, such as YouTube (videos) and Flickr (photos), all supported by nimble and interactive information technology infrastructures (Bollier, 2008; Collins, Morgan, & Patrinos, 2003; Hess & Ostrom, 2007; Lessig, 2001).

As will be described in more detail, InCommons uses new technologies to enable the sharing of diverse knowledge resources useful to community-based leaders. The theory of action presumes this type of knowledge is abundant. Existing institutions and incentives, however, provide few opportunities to share and benefit from what is learned when leaders, for example, improve water quality in the river running through their town, help their community integrate new Americans, or develop safe places for their youth to gather after school. By encouraging people to see this type of practical knowledge as valuable (and thus worthy of being shared), creating a platform that decreases the costs of such sharing, and stressing open access and transparency, a knowledge commons is being created (Benkler, 2006; Bollier, 2008; Ghosh, 2007). Theoretically, assumes participants have some level of self-interest and InCommons capitalizes on it by tapping the human desire to be recognized and validated for hard-earned insights from leadership experiences.

Proposition #3: Creating twenty-first century spaces for civic engagement supports the process of complex community change.

Community-based leadership does not depend on positional authority, rather it emerges from complex interactions within particular contexts (Pigg, 1999). The interactions among people, the rules at play, and everyday chance encounters can significantly determine the direction and outcomes of change efforts. Particular events often are highly interdependent and effective leadership capitalizes on the dynamics of complex systems (Hazy, Goldstein, & Lichtenstein, 2007; Jennings & Dooley, 2007; Marion & Uhl-Bien, 2001; Paarlberg & Bielefeld, 2009; Wheatley, 2006). In these situations, opportunities for dialog and deliberation are quite significant. They can create the conditions where positive change can unfold.

Free, public space, where citizens gather to discuss and debate the most pressing issues of the day and make collective judgments, is a foundational concept in modern democracies. Yet, today many people worry that these norms of dialog and deliberation, of collective responsibility and accountability, have significantly deteriorated, fueling political polarization (Block, 2009). Free spaces existing between our private lives and large-scale institutions provide settings where people can learn public skills, civic values, and establish deeper group identity (Boyte, 2004; Evans & Boyte, 1986). They provide opportunities to gather, away from home or work, to establish connections and deliberate, and to understand both what holds us together and creates discord. The interactive internet also offers ways to reinforce face-to-face free spaces. As longtime internet observer Phil Agre describes, "Face-to-face meetings will always be indispensable for cementing relationships and sharing worldviews, but the internet is valuable before and after those meetings" (cited in London, 2007, p. 3). A large-scale initiative like InCommons focused on supporting community leaders is using such insights and new capabilities to seed systemic change.

These propositions, as part of a larger InCommons theory of action, explicitly and implicitly guided program planning and implementation and helped structure a chain of events (Patton, 1986, 2002).

Core values and developmental strategies

The results of the initial research were reviewed, examined, and debated with the institutional partners, helping to refine a theory of action and shape an emerging initiative. The partners developed a business plan and agreed that staffing would not all be paid with foundation grants. Instead, partner institutions would dedicate time to developing and implementing specific elements of the plan. The initiative name, InCommons, was selected to stress the collective benefit of sharing and receiving from others. Responding to leaders' articulated needs for a long-term commitment, transparency, and co-creation, a four-phase development framework was developed to engage others: Introduction and awareness building (2010–2011); awareness building, testing, and refinement (2011); statewide growth (2012); and developing a multistate scale (2013 and beyond).

At the outset, all institutional partners agreed to core principles: InCommons would focus on state and local community issues, creating opportunities for participants to have new experiences that pushed boundaries and built trust. The initiative would strengthen social networks by both improving access to practical knowledge and resources, and building skills and experience with authentic community engagement. Partners agreed to align their ongoing events and activities, such as conferences, training programs, community meetings, and to have larger impact. Partners would help identify and tell the stories of individuals demonstrating community leadership. Most importantly, partner institutions would share owner-ship with community leaders and focus on unleashing this grassroots power rather than enhancing their own institutional position.

Consistent with the theory of action, several strategies were developed: Web-based *resource sharing* and *idea competitions* focus on sharing and elevating the practical knowledge of community leaders. *Gatherings* and *building capacity for uncommon conversations* focus on creating spaces, where community concerns can be explored and solutions developed.

Sharing web-based resources

Applying Ostrom's concept of common-pool resources, a unique web platform to find and share practical resources relevant to community problem solving was created. Combining the functionality of social networking and resource aggregation, a beta version of InCommons.org was launched in late 2010. People use the platform to find and offer resources, ideas, and best practices. After creating a profile, they can join discussion groups, ask specific questions, and locate tools and resources that might help in their situation. Since launch, the website has received a monthly average of over 5800 visits.

In assessing other commons-based peer production sites, Benkler (2006) points out that sites have two evolutionary phases – creating the content and focusing on quality assurance. Attending to creating and populating web content is important at first to respond to initial users' needs, establish relevance, and motivate participation (Lui & Sandfort, 2011). For InCommons, institutional partners initially took the lead in finding, developing, and sharing relevant resources on the website (e.g. links to ongoing training programs, relevant media stories, abridged summaries of research articles). Substantive topics were prioritized based on pressing challenges and community interest – obesity, public budgeting, and youth programming – and partners excavated relevant resources from within their institutions. They also listened to research informants, attendees at face-to-face gatherings, and individuals identified by the partners, developing specific resources relevant to their needs. Rather than a typical one-to-one technical assistance model, the institutions shared identified resources at the InCommons website, enabling others to access them. To date, more than 650 resources about diverse topics are shared in this way.

The first phase, also identified people comfortable sharing ideas, resources, and questions virtually. In moving to subsequent phases, there are expectations that users of the on-line resources will also become resource contributors. The initiative's brand, web narrative, and highlighted leadership stories all communicate a message about participation in the new community of purpose. The first phase resources are high quality and relevant to improve confidence of the knowledge commons. Site features also invite participation and co-creation; if a user searches on a topic with no existing resources, they are invited to pose a question to the online community, to generate more helpful responses. To date, over 6500 people have profiles enabling them to share resources and benefit from the InCommons online community.

Enabling idea competitions

Another strategy intended to enhance online engagement involves using a competition to recognize innovation and engage citizens in developing solutions to collective problems (Berger, 2008). Referenced in the popular literature as "ideagoras" (Tapscott & Williams, 2006), the idea competitions have gained prominence in recent years as corporations, foundations, and the media leverage the power of the internet to capture innovative ideas on a grand scale. One of InCommons' institutional partners, the international non-profit Ashoka, has successfully run many such competitions on its website and their expertise benefited the project.

To date, InCommons has hosted seven idea competitions focusing on diverse challenges, such as reducing obesity, expanding multicultural programming, preserving water quality, and promoting innovative environmental initiatives. Calls for participation are prepared and people are encouraged to submit ideas or innovations that successfully address that challenge. When ideas or projects are nominated, others can comment to enhance, critique, or offer suggestions. Most competitions also use wide citizen participation, or "crowd sourcing," to narrow ideas or select final winners. Winners receive professional recognition or a modest financial prize.

For private corporations or foundations, the platforms' ability to engage diverse participants in the online community, publicize innovative ideas, and reduce staff time reviewing proposals are all appealing. As Judith Rodin, President of the Rockefeller Foundation explained, "At [the competition site] all of the solutions are posted so that everyone can read them and perhaps build on one another's solutions. They are not in the same room, but they can collaborate virtually, making it possible to create a different and better solution" (Nee, 2009, p. 14). In the past year, Minnesotans have generated over 920 ideas and tens of thousands have participated in online voting to identify semi-finalists or winners in the seven competitions. The submissions become additional shared resources in the virtual community, as people can learn of others already making progress on complex community issues. Although motivated by the potential of winning and the recognition or financial benefits, the ideas and program descriptions become potent, collective resources to elevate the work of everyday leaders, and make it more accessible to all.

Crafting unusual gatherings

While the initiative uses the virtual tools of the interactive web to support and inspire knowledge sharing, it also stresses the essential role of face-to-face connections in making progress on important issues. InCommons gatherings are in-person con- venings, meetings, and events where people are invited to listen, learn, and strategize about action. They differ from typical meetings or conferences in intent and process.

All InCommons gatherings cultivate a sense of respect, belonging, and responsibility for co-creation. They are designed by trained facilitators to reflect a clear purpose but no predetermined outcome, using proven methods to engage people with a diversity of perspectives. High-quality relevant information, such as objective data, scientific evidence, or case studies, aids in deliberations. Evocative tools, such as art, music, metaphor, or physical movements are used to inspire creativity and new awareness. Coming out of each gathering, a product or story is harvested to document the progress that occurred and allow information to be shared virtually for those not present. Care is paid to simple hospitality, assuring that physical and social barriers to participation are removed and high-quality logistics, space, and refreshments exist to support the work.

The University of Minnesota hosted one of the first InCommons gatherings in October 2010. *Connecting community leaders for renewal and action* brought together graduates from nine different university-based leadership programs. Program participants from school districts, city and county governments, media, and non-profit organizations were invited from targeted geographic areas across the state. In keeping with InCommons gatherings principles, the agenda had a clear three-part purpose: Strengthen a network of leaders across multiple sectors, connect communities to InCommons resources, and inspire participants to engage others across sectors in their communities. The actual gathering agenda, though, was co-created by participants. In a two-day facilitated session, participants identified and discussed the most pressing issues in their communities and explored how they might benefit from engagement with InCommons and the University. The conversation topics were broad, ranging from assuring smooth transitions for school-aged children to enhancing rural economic development, protecting water quality to privatizing public service. Conference themes, insights, and tools were harvested and made available to others on the initiative website. In addition, staff followed up with each participant to learn more about these leaders' ongoing needs, respond to specific informational requests, and encourage resource sharing among participants via InCommons.org.

Other, InCommons gatherings have brought together other alumni from leadership programs or focused on specific topical areas: Healthcare access, racial disparities in education, rural economic development, environmental sustainability, and the state's budget crisis. To support high quality convenings across these topics, the initiative has focused on building facilitators' capacities to design gatherings that are purpose-driven and impactful.

Building capacity to host uncommon conversations

The needs assessment stressed the importance of improving people's abilities to engage others in addressing community concerns. To do so, we identified a core of common practices, the "Art of Hosting," (Art of Hosting, 2011; Block, 2009; Holman, 2010) which facilitators could use to design and facilitate gatherings in ways consistent with community needs or presenting situation. In fact, the Art of Hosting provides an operating system for InCommons gatherings consistent with the proposition that complex community change requires both structured and nimble process support. Like open source computer programmers who share code, Art of Hosting practitioners freely shares process tools designed to work within complex human systems.

In fact, there is an international Art of Hosting community of practice (Wenger, 1998). Members apply these techniques in diverse contexts, focusing on youth employment, economic development, indigenous people's rights, and European Union governance. Columbus, Ohio has used Art of Hosting strategies as part of re-envisioning health care, higher education, business networks, and social services in that community (Frieze & Wheatley, 2011). These experiences and lessons learned are shared with other facilitators working in this international community of practice.

The Art of Hosting process of design and implementation views change as occurring in complex, dynamic systems. By posing provocative questions to people convened around a specific purpose or topic and supporting them with engaging facilitation practices, the approach yields significant advances in collective under-standing. The Art of Hosting process is also driven by a belief that individuals are more committed to change if they see themselves as contributors in planning discussions and decisions. Some core hosting practices include circle dialog, appreciative inquiry, open space technology, and world café (Baldwin & Linnea, 2010; Brown & Isaacs, 2005; Cooperrider & Whitney, 2000; Owen, 1997), but new techniques are continually being developed by community members. The Art of Hosting integrates these techniques and encourages facilitators to select processes consistent with the presenting issues and contexts. However, in Hosting, facilitators do not merely use these techniques to advance a predetermined agenda. Rather, techniques are selected and employed to elicit the resources and abilities inherent in the community gathered. When paired with on-line resource sharing, the Art of Hosting creates the potential for broadening the impact of InCommons.

InCommons is currently building Minnesota's Art of Hosting community of practice as a strategy to expand capacity to host gatherings at a larger scale.

Experienced facilitators receive three or four complimentary days of training and, in return, offer an equivalent number of facilitation days pro bono to InCommons gatherings. To date, we have trained over 150 facilitators and are conducting research on their longer-term practice using the engagement methods. Trained facilitators communicate regularly, in-person and virtually, work together on projects, and share their learning, thus mirroring the learning community envisioned for the larger InCommons initiative.

Analyzing early implementation

Consistent with the PAR approach, we can now turn back to criteria generated during the needs assessment phase to assess early implementation of this community leadership initiative. In initial interviews with 65 formal and informal leaders, participants expressed excitement and apprehension. In particular, they noted the significant risk involved when philanthropic institutions employ such a systems change strategy. Many stakeholders experienced a very real loss when a trusted philanthropic funder moved away from deploying financial resources to impose mandates, induce change, or build pre-determined capacity. For a systems change initiative to work, stakeholders stressed the importance of the initiative having a *visible presence in communities* and the need for partners to demonstrate a *long-term commitment*. They asked that InCommons operate with *transparency and credibility* and assure *co-creation and shared ownership* in the true spirit of a commons.

These characteristics shaped the emerging theory of action and encouraged use of particular strategies. Table 2 summarizes these desired characteristics, further describes their attributes and how they relate to the dimensions in the theory of action. It also illustrates how the first phase of InCommons has demonstrated these aspirations. For example, members of a gatherings working group pay considerable attention to identifying potential facilitators to be trained who have knowledge of and experience with diverse settings, to allow InCommons to be rooted in community issues. In addition, the internet platform provides transparency in providing resources, such as research translation and process tools, and outcomes from InCommons gatherings.

We have made progress consistent with leaders' desires – creating a genuine presence in community, promoting the effort over time with a phased approach, using credible sources and technology to be transparent, and adjusting tactics in the spirit of co-creation.

Yet, there are other ways the initiative does not yet fulfill the aspirations of the theory of action. For one, while the theory acknowledges the ambiguity of systems change, these conditions are difficult to weather. While many stakeholders recognize the need and appreciate the value of community-defined goals, they also struggle to change their behaviors. Some of these challenges arise from lack of experience with a large scale self-generating community like InCommons. Large institutions are accustomed to being accountable to sponsor-funded initiatives and can lose sight of InCommons operational details in the absence of grant responsibilities. Some individuals question whether their experiences with solving problems are sufficiently worthy to be shared with others. Some facilitators worry about sharing failures with others through their community of practice because they are unaccustomed to that level of professional vulnerability. InCommons is

Table 2. Community-based leaders desired characteristics of InCommons*.

Desired characteristics and attributes	Illustrative activities	Relevance to theory of action
Genuine presence in community: Rooted in local experiences and non-partisan focused on making change	• Develop range of web-based resources and applications open to all • Illuminate stories of courageous leaders to inspire others • Concentrate efforts in some geographic places and ethnic communities • Involve diverse facilitators in training and community of practice to support gatherings	Sharing knowledge resources Creating spaces for community change
Promote over time: Embracing non-linear change processes with long-time horizon	• Adopt phased approach using multiple strategies • Sponsor idea competitions and follow-up, promoting and supporting finalists	Funders relinquishing some control Creating spaces for community change
Transparency and credibility: Operated without regard to institutional, cultural, or geographic boundaries; promoting quality resources and gatherings	• Use new information technologies to share knowledge and reinforce social networks • Involve respected institutions as institutional partners to help curate web-content • Adopt high quality facilitation practices and ongoing support for practice	Funders relinquishing some control Sharing knowledge resources Creating spaces for community change
Co-creation and shared ownership: Soliciting feedback and evolving because of feedback from contributors	• Ongoing improvements to functionality of website • Enable facilitators to shape ongoing community of practice	Funders relinquishing some control Sharing knowledge resources

Note: *Developed through an analysis of semi-structured interviews with over 65 informants consulted during initiative development.

asking people to operate from a fundamentally different paradigm from conventional public affairs work.

Another challenge comes from the inherent tension between the initiative's commitment to community realities and its statewide reach. Individuals have particular experiences with InCommons: They observe the state's public radio station being more engaged in local issues, attend a gathering on a timely public policy issue, or find relevant resources on-line. They are inspired when voting in an idea competition, enjoy recognition as a competition semi-finalist, or find their own facilitation practice changed because of training they've received.

Yet, it is difficult for them to see the initiative as larger than these particular experiences (Aman, 2011). Because of the commitment to shared ownership, the institutional partners have hesitated to define InCommons beyond its goal of supporting courageous community leadership. But this has created some governance and structural challenges. The research on knowledge commons development stresses that clear governance and operational rules are important to encourage contribution, sharing, and guarantee protection of resources (Bollier, 2008; Hess & Ostrom, 2007; Lessig, 2001). Yet, operational concerns, such as website functionality and communications, have occupied disproportionate staff and institutional partners' attention. Long-term sustainability likely will hinge on instituting clearer governance and "rules in use" about sharing and using community resources.

Finally, while many people hunger for a setting where they can engage in deep dialog on important issues, others are calling for immediate action. People feel pressure to move quickly to find solutions and demonstrate results, even in the face of a divergent understanding of problems, change strategies, and desirable outcomes. InCommons gatherings slow people down. As Toke Moeller, one of the Art of Hosting founders often says, "You need to go slow in order to go fast." Yet most people are not used to spaces where uncommon conversations occur, differing worldviews interact, and more fundamental change can grow. While some InCommons gatherings bring people together who quickly agree about the problem, solution, and act to resolve the issue, often initial gatherings are just the beginning of the change process. What is needed is a longer-term process of listening, challenging, and reframing issues to allow better solutions to emerge. This type of leadership takes time, patience, and courage (Block, 2009; Holman, 2010). It is central to the mission of InCommons.

As researchers, we are continually using the theory of action with partners to deepen a collective understanding of the benefits and pitfalls of creating this community-based leadership commons. Use of PAR approach, both produces evidence about an ongoing process of change and promotes formative learning among the stakeholders closest to the work. While still in the initial phases, there are some implications for others interested in fostering community-based leadership development.

Implications for community-based leadership development and further inquiry

The InCommons initiative is a new model of community-leadership development. It is a systems change initiative designed to inspire and support the courageous leadership needed to engage communities and solve problems. It leverages the power of the interactive web to share and generate practical knowledge abundant in communities, while at the same time cultivating a new level of intentionality and impact in face-to-face gatherings.

These strategies are distinct, yet complimentary to the more traditional cohort-based CLPs. Such programs can be powerful for participants. But often it is difficult for others not present to benefit or even understand the type of change created in those programs. InCommons clearly operates at a larger scale and future evaluation and research will document the mechanisms of influence present.

However, the theory of action suggests by sharing and connecting others, we will change the dominant social narrative that leadership is scarce. Every day acts of leadership show that it actually is abundant. In the current social environment infused with cynicism, this type of message and reframing of experience is important. By describing the underlying theory of action and assessing initial development of

InCommons, we hope others will be encouraged to seek promising new approaches to bolstering leadership at large scale in communities.

InCommons is still in its initial phase of development (introduction and awareness building) and the jury is still out on its long-term sustainability, impact, and replicability. Up to this point, the PAR has been intentionally inclusive, designed to incorporate community stakeholders' multiple perspectives about early success indicators during this first phase. As InCommons matures, evaluation efforts must keep pace and balance such inclusiveness with an ability to measure the sustained impact of a broad-scale initiative, where both strategies and desired outcomes may manifest themselves in different ways across different communities. This will likely entail blending the PAR strategies and developmental approach (Patton, 2007) with a deeper focus on cluster evaluation and measuring consistent indicators of replicability (Kellogg Foundation, 2007), regardless of specific community-level outcomes identified by specific community-level stakeholders. Measuring the durability of the underlying construct of *leadership as an abundant resource inherent in communities* will remain a constant element of InCommons evaluation.

References

Aman, J. (2011). *InCommons: Creating seeds of change. Evaluation report.* Minneapolis, MN: Public & Nonprofit Leadership Center, Humphrey School, University of Minnesota.

Art of Hosting. (2011). Retrieved from http://www.artofhosting.com

Bailin, M. (2004). *Philanthropy in practice: Great expectations versus getting the job done.* State of Philanthropy 2004. Washington, DC: National Committee for Responsive Philanthropy.

Baldwin, C., & Linnea, A. (2010). *The circle way: A leaders in every chair.* San Francisco, CA: Berrett-Koehler.

Benkler, Y. (2006). *The wealth of networks: How social production transforms markets and freedom.* New Haven, CT: Yale University Press.

Berger, L. (2008). How changemakers' "collaborative competitions" harness the wisdom of crowds. *Stanford Social Innovation Review, 6*(1), 67–68.

Bickman, L. (1987). The functions of program theory. *New Directions for Program Evaluation, 33,* 5–18.

Block, P. (2009). *Community: The structure of belonging.* New York: Berrett-Koehler.

Bollier, D. (2007). The growth of the commons paradigm. In *Understanding knowledge as a commons: From theory to practice* (pp. 27–40). Cambridge, MA: MIT.

Bollier, D. (2008). *Viral spiral: How the commoners built a digital republic of their own.* New York, NY: The New Press.

Boyte, H. (2004). *Everyday politics: Reconnecting citizens and public life.* Philadelphia, PA: University of Pennsylvania.

Boyte, H. (2011). Free spaces and civil society. In M. Edwards (Ed.), *Oxford handbook on civil society* (pp. 343–362). London: Oxford University Press.

Brown, E., Fleetham, S., Shurilla, A., & Simonson, D. (2010). *What do courageous leaders need to be effective?* Unpublished master's of public policy, Humphrey School of Public Affairs, University of Minnesota, Minneapolis, MN.

Brown, J., & Isaacs, D. (2005). *The world café: Shaping our futures through conversations that matter.* San Francisco, CA: Berrett-Koehler.

Brown, R.B., & Nylander, A.B. (1998). Community leadership structure: Differences between rural community leaders' and residents' informational networks. *Journal of the Community Development Society, 29*(1), 71.

Burns, J.M. (2003). *Transforming leadership: A new pursuit of happiness.* New York: Atlantic Monthly Press.

Chazdon, S.A., & Lott, S. (2010). Ready for engagement: Using key informant interviews to measure community social capacity. *Community Development, 41,* 156.

Cohen, M., & March, J. (1974). *Leadership and ambiguity: The American college president.* New York: McGraw-Hill.

Collins, F.S., Morgan, M., & Patrinos, A. (2003). The human genome project: Lessons from large-scale biology. *Science, 300,* 286–290.

Cooperrider, D., & Whitney, D. (2000). *Appreciative inquiry: A positive revolution in change.* San Francisco, CA: Berrett-Koehler.

Crosby, B.C., & Bryson, J.M. (2005). *Leadership for the common good: Tackling public problems in a shared-power world.* San Francisco, CA: Jossey-Bass.

Daloz, L.P., Keen, C., Keen, J., & Parks, S.D. (1996). *Common fire: Leading lives of commitment in a complex world.* Boston, MA: Beacon Press.

Dietz, T., Ostrom, E., & Stern, P. (2003). The struggle to govern the commons. *Science, 302,* 1907–1912.

Earl, J. (2007). Leading acts in a leaderless movement. *American Behavioral Scientist, 50,* 1327–1349.

Emery, M., Fernandez, E., Gutierrez-Montes, I., & Butler Flora, C. (2007). *Leadership as community capacity building: A study on the impact of leadership development training on community.* New York: Routledge.

Evans, S.M., & Boyte, H. (1986). *Free spaces: The sources of democratic change in America.* New York: Harper & Row.

Frieze, D., & Wheatley, M. (2011). From hero to host: A story of citizenship in Columbus, Ohio. In M. Wheatley & D. Frieze (Eds.), *Walk out, walk on: A learning journey into communities daring to live the future now* (pp. 188–215). New York: BK Currents.

Frumkin, P. (2006). *Strategic giving: The art and science of philanthropy.* Chicago, IL: University of Chicago Press.

Fulton, K., & Blau, A. (2005). *Looking out for the future: An orientation for twenty-first century philanthropists.* Cambridge, MA: Global Business Network.

Ghosh, S. (2007). How to build a commons: Is intellectual property constrictive, facilitating, or irrelevant? In C. Hess & E. Ostrom (Eds.), *Understanding knowledge as a commons: From theory to practice* (pp. 209–245). Cambridge, MA: MIT.

Gira, E.C., Kessler, M.L., & Poertner, J. (2004). Influencing social workers to use research evidence in practice: Lessons from medicine and the allied health professions. *Research on Social Work Practice, 14,* 68–79.

Grassroots Solutions. (2010, April). *Engagement audit findings.* St. Paul, MN: Grassroots Solutions.

Hardin, G. (1968). The tragedy of the commons. *Science, 162,* 1243–1248.

Hazy, J., Goldstein, J., & Lichtenstein, B. (2007). Complex systems leadership theory: An introduction. In J. Hazy, J. Goldstein & B. Lichtenstein (Eds.), *Complex systems leadership theory: New perspectives from complexity science on social and organizational effectiveness* (pp. 1–13). Mansfield, MA: ISCE Publishing.

Heifetz, R.A., Kania, J.V., & Kramer, M.R. (2004). Leading boldly. *Stanford Social Innovation Review, 2,* 21–31.

Hess, C., & Ostrom, E. (Eds.). (2007). *Understanding knowledge as a commons: From theory to practice.* Cambridge, MA: MIT.

Holman, P. (2010). *Engaging emergence: Turning upheaval into opportunity.* New York: Berrett-Koehler.

Jennings, P.L., & Dooley, K.J. (2007). An emerging complexity paradigm in leadership research. In J. Hazy, J. Goldstein & B. Lichtenstein (Eds.), *Complex systems leadership theory: New perspectives from complexity science on social and organizational effectiveness* (pp. 17–34). Mansfield, MA: ISCE Publishing.

Kellogg Foundation. (2007). *Designing initiative evaluation: A systems-oriented framework for evaluating social change efforts.* Battle Creek, MI: W.K. Kellogg Foundation.

Kouzes, J.M., & Posner, B.Z. (2007). *The leadership challenge* (4th ed.). San Francisco, CA: John Wiley & Sons.

Lam, W.F., & Ostrom, E. (2010). Lessons from the dynamic complexity of development interventions: Lessons from an irrigation experiment in Nepal. *Journal of Policy Analysis & Management, 43,* 1–25.

Lessig, L. (2001). *The future of ideas: The fate of the commons in a connected world.* New York: Random House.

Lewins, A., & Silver, C. (2007). *Using software in qualitative research: A step-by-step guide.* Thousand Oaks, CA: Sage Publications.

Lohmann, R.A. (1992). *The commons: New perspectives on nonprofit organizations and voluntary action*. San Francisco, CA: Jossey-Bass.

London, S. (2007). Civic networks: Building community on the net. In R. Norgaard (Ed.), *Composing knowledge* (pp. 186–201). New York: Bedford/St. Martins.

Lui, H., & Sandfort, J.R. (2011). Open source platforms for citizen engagement: Examining Ashoka's design and implementation. *Nonprofit Policy Forum*.

Mandell, J. (2010). Picnics, participation and power: Linking community building to social change. *Community Development, 41*, 269.

Marion, R., & Uhl-Bien, M. (2001). Leadership in complex organizations. *Leadership Quarterly, 12*, 389.

McDonnell, L., & Elmore, R. (1987). Getting the job done: Alternative policy instruments. *Educational Administration and Policy Analysis, 9*, 133–152.

McIntyre, R. (2008). *Participatory action research*. Thousand Oaks, CA: Sage Publications.

McKersie, W.S. (1999). Local philanthropy matters: Pressing issues for research and practice. In E. Condliffe Lagemann (Ed.), *Philanthropic foundations: New scholarship new possibilities* (pp. 329–358). Bloomington and Indianapolis, IN: Indiana University Press.

McTaggart, R. (1997). *Participatory action research: International contexts and consequences*. Albany, NY: State University of New York Press.

Nee, E. (2009). Q&A: Judith Rodin. *Stanford Social Innovation Review, 2*(2), 1–20. Retrieved from http://www.ssireview.org/articles/entry/q_a_judith_rodin/

Nohria, N., & Khurana, R. (Eds.). (2010). *Handbook of leadership theory and practice*. Boston, MA: Harvard Business Press.

Ostrom, E. (1990). *Governing the commons: The evolutions of institutions for collective action*. Cambridge: Cambridge University Press.

Ostrom, E. (2010). Beyond markets and states: Polycentric governance of complex economic systems. *American Economic Review, 100*, 641–672.

Owen, H. (1997). *Open space technology: A user's guide*. San Francisco, CA: Berrett-Koehler.

Paarlberg, L., & Bielefeld, W. (2009). Complexity science – An alternative framework for understanding strategic management in public serving organizations. *International Public Management Journal, 12*, 236–260.

Parks, S.D. (2005). *Leadership can be taught: A bold approach for a complex world*. Cambridge, MA: Harvard Business School Press.

Patton, M.Q. (1986). *Utilization-focused research*. Thousands Oaks, CA: Sage Publications.

Patton, M.Q. (2002). *Qualitative research and evaluation methods*. Thousands Oaks, CA: Sage Publications.

Patton, M.Q. (2007). Evaluation for the way we work. *The Nonprofit Quarterly, 13*(1), 28–33.

Pigg, K.E. (1999). Community leadership and community theory: A practical synthesis. *Journal of the Community Development Society, 30*, 196.

Poteete, A.R., Janssen, M.A., & Ostrom, E. (2010). *Working together: Collective action, the commons, and multiple methods in practice*. Princeton, NJ: Princeton University Press.

Public Strategies Group. (2009). *Leadership for the 21st century: A catalytic strategy*. St. Paul, MN. Retrieved from: http://www1.umn.edu/pres/bush/docs/Design%20Lab%20Pub%20 Final.pdf

Rausch, E., & MartinRogers, N. (2010). *Developing courageous leaders and engaging communities in solving problems*. St. Paul, MN: Wilder Research Center. Retrieved from http://www.wilder.org/download.0.html?report=2317

Sandfort, J.R. (2008). Using lessons from public affairs to inform strategic philanthropy. *Nonprofit & Voluntary Sector Quarterly, 37*, 537–552.

Senge, P., Scharmer, C.O., Jaworski, J., & Flowers, B.S. (2004). *Presence: An exploration of profound change in people, organizations, and society*. New York: Currency Doubleday.

Silver, I. (2004). Negotiating the antipoverty agenda: Foundations, community organizations, and comprehensive community initiatives. *Nonprofit and Voluntary Sector Quarterly, 33*, 606–627.

Tapscott, D., & Williams, A.D. (2006). *Wikinomics: How mass collaboration changes everything*. New York: Portfolio.

Thomas, A.B. (1988). Does leadership make a difference to organizational performance? *Administrative Science Quarterly, 33*, 388–400.

Weiss, C.H. (1995). Nothing as practical as good theory: Exploring theory based evaluation for comprehensive community initiatives for children and families. *Approaches to Evaluating Community Initiatives, 65,* 123–142.

Wenger, E. (1998). *Communities of practice: Learning, meaning and identity.* New York: Cambridge University Press.

Wheatley, M. (2006). *Leadership and the new science: Discovering order in a chaotic world* (3rd ed.). San Francisco, CA: Berrett-Koehler.

Wilder Research Center. (2009). *Developing courageous leaders and engaging entire communities in solving problems: 2009 household survey in Minnesota, North Dakota, and South Dakota.* St. Paul, MN: Wilder Research Center.

Wituk, S., Ealey, S., Clark, M.J., Heiny, P., & Meissen, G. (2005). Community development through community leadership programs: Insights from a statewide community leadership initiative. *Community Development, 36,* 89–101.

Community leadership development education: promoting civic engagement through human and social capital

Godwin T. Apaliyah[a], Kenneth E. Martin[b], Stephen P. Gasteyer[c], Kari Keating[d] and Kenneth Pigg[e]

[a]Rural Sociology Program, School of Environment and Natural Resources, The Ohio State University, Columbus, USA; [b]Department of Extension, The Ohio State University, USA; [c]Department of Sociology, Michigan State University, East Lansing, USA; [d]Department of Human and Community Development, University of Illinois, Urbana-Champaign, USA; [e]Department of Rural Sociology, University of Missouri, Columbia, USA

Community leadership development education (CLDE) programs are designed to increase the capacity of individuals as leaders in their communities as well as increase the capacity of community leadership as a whole. These programs contribute to building a critical mass of individuals in the community by developing their leadership skills and knowledge to be effective leaders. However, there is little research that connects characteristics of individual leadership skills to increased capacity for community development. The article addresses this by looking at how CLDE programs contribute to building and enhancing the human capital and social capital of program participants and how these benefits lead to human capital and social capital benefits in the community as well as improvements in the other five community capitals – cultural, political, built, natural, and financial.

Introduction

For rural communities, the twenty-first century has brought many challenges. Forces of globalization have forced upon communities (either through inclusion or omission) new problems, opportunities, and ways of being. Rural community residents live in places where the traditional identities of place are in transition. Not only have old industries closed doors, but the demographics are aging and communities often face challenges of development not only with fewer wealthy residents but also dwindling populations overall. Economic development is often marked by new industries, new technologies, and increased competition for accessing technologies and industries, and the knowledge of how to utilize them for the betterment of communities (Brown & Schafft, 2011). At worst, community residents are struggling as mills, mines, factories, and surrounding farmers have left or dwindled in numbers.

Further, with government devolution of services provision, communities have to address issues ranging from local poverty to environmental quality (Sharp & Parisi, 2003). It is not surprising, then, that there has been a resurgence in literature on the development of community and civic capacity (Block, 2008; Hyman, 2002; Saegert, 2006) and community empowerment (Pigg, 2002).

Rural communities often face two major challenges as they attempt to compete for economic opportunities, improve quality of life, and address emerging issues. Precisely, because of the process of youth "brain drain," rural communities face real challenges in human capital or the suite of skills, knowledge, and abilities at the community level (Flora & Flora, 2008; Green & Haines, 2007). One of the challenges in human capital is often measured in terms of education levels – such as the percent of college educated people or the percent of technically trained people who can perform certain skills. A second challenge to human capital pertains to the extent to which communities have members who can negotiate increasingly complicated application and proposal processes for grant or loan funding or who know how to contact their legislator to ask for the special tax status to lure an industry or put on a new wing of the local hospital. Even more basic, do the leaders in a community know how to run a meeting, to convene a community decision-making process, or to make sure that stakeholders in the community are appropriately included in decision-making processes? Further, are people with human capital in a community recognized and included in development processes (Flora & Flora, 2008; Green & Haines, 2007)?

While having and recognizing skills sets is important, resources and opportunities available to rural communities are also often difficult to access. Dating to the early 1990s, the notion of social capital (relationships of trust and reciprocity) has received increasing attention, especially in the context of rural development (Flora & Flora, 2008; Schafft & Brown, 2003). The development of the concept has led to a distinction between two types of social capital (Putnam, 2000). Bonding social capital involves relationships among a well-acquainted and similar group of individuals that may be exclusionary of others. Bridging social capital involves relationships outside of the well-acquainted group. Ideally, there is a balance among these types of social capital, leading to reaffirming relationships with close friends, neighbors and family, and relationships that bring in the new ideas that come with exposure to other people and institutions (Flora & Flora, 2008).

Human capital and social capital are very much related. Having existing skills, knowledge, and self-efficacy can open doors to certain social networks. For instance, trained water operators may come to know about opportunities for community infrastructure development through relationships with other operators in the state (e.g. social capital). At the same time, high levels of bridging and bonding social capital can be critical to identifying and leveraging existing human capital. In addition, there is some evidence that higher levels of bridging social capital increase civic capacity in the community and the ability to increase the well-being of residents (Orum & Gramlich, 1999; Wagner, 2004). For Emery, Fernandez, Gutierrez-Montes, and Flora (2007), among the key reasons behind the growth of leadership training in rural areas has been an effort to build community capacity through trainings that increased both human and social capital: "Leadership training programs ... provide emerging leaders with experiences that will strengthen ... capacity by strengthening their knowledge, skills, and self-efficacy (human capital) and ... increasing their access to networks and resources (social and political capital)"(p. 62). Rasmussen, Armstrong, and Chazdon (2011) also address the importance of bridging social capital as an important aspect of a community leadership development education (CLDE) program and relate this factor directly to creating more effective civic actors in the community. Emery et al. (2007) note that "respondents relied on their new bridging social capital to identify resources that led to successful efforts to build [capacity]" (p. 64). In other words, leadership development programs may be an important mechanism to build these two critical assets for aspiring leaders. Most of these leadership programs are community-based and the agendas are controlled by community residents who are concerned about the leadership capacity of their communities and where their communities are headed. This article will test empirically the extent to which individual-level and community-level human and social capital are created or strengthened through community leadership and education programs.

Leadership education programs

Most of the research on leadership over the past 40 years has focused on large, complex organizations such as businesses, governments, and the military (Rost, 1993). There is limited research on leadership in the community context and that research has tended to look at the benefits of leadership for individual participants with an emphasis on personal and inter-personal skills and knowledge.

The research question, this article addresses is whether CLDE programs that produce immediate individual effects also result in community effects. CLDE programs contribute to two of the seven leadership development models described by the University of Michigan School of Social Work (2007). They support the individual skills/capacity building model by providing training for skills and knowledge development. This is supported in the Phase I analysis reported below, where human and social capital benefits are documented for the program participants using six outcome indices. CLDE programs also contribute to the grassroots community model by identifying, training, and supporting community participants as they prepare for leadership roles in developing solutions to carry out their vision for positively impacting the community. This is supported in the Phase II analysis, where CLDE program participants take on leadership roles in activities and projects that benefit the community by strengthening one or more of seven community capitals.

CLDE programs are often used to develop and increase the capacity of individuals as leaders in their communities as well as contribute to the capacity of community leadership as a whole. CLDE programs generally follow the academy model, where a group of people commit to participate in the program for a period of time for intensive learning. Sponsors may include chambers of commerce, community colleges and four-year colleges, university extension, and private foundations. These programs contribute to building a critical mass of individuals in the community by developing their leadership skills and knowledge to be effective leaders. The anticipated results include improvements in individual skills, increased knowledge about the community, and strengthened social networks. The resultant cadre of local leaders should help to make community development efforts more effective.

In the CLDE program evaluation literature, there is a body of research that documents training effects on individuals (Black & Earnest, 2009; Brundgardt & Seibel, 1995; Earnest, 1996; Langone, 1992; Pigg, 1990, 2001; Rohs & Langone, 1993). Other research has focused on differences in participant outcomes

(Dhanakumar, Rossing, & Campbell, 1996; Whent & Leising, 1992). There is also limited research on community-level effects (Black & Earnest, 2009; Emery et al., 2007; Emery & Flora, 2006). However, there is little research that connects characteristics of individual leadership skills to increased capacity for community development. The research presented here addresses this by looking at how CLDE programs contribute not only to improving individual leadership skills but also to community development by building and enhancing one or more of seven community capitals as CLDE program participants take on leadership roles in activities and projects for the benefit of the community.

The community capitals framework (CCF), developed by Emery, Fey, and Flora (2006), Green and Haines (2007), and others, provides a flexible framework for examining the contributions of CLDE program participants to community development initiatives and activities. The CCF represents the diversity of community resources as "capitals" in a manner similar to that used by economists to describe capital assets except that the CCF extends the notion of capital to include non-financial forms. The seven CCF capitals are represented as: natural, cultural, social, human, political, financial, and built capitals. Each of these capital categories is considered distinct but related in that leveraging one (or more) form of capital can be instrumental in increasing the stock of another capital form. The CCF is not presented as a theory of community development in the discussion represented here although there are certainly implications in this regard for theory development. Rather, the CCF is used as a guide to organizing information gathered about the nature of collective actions taken, the shared purposes to be achieved, and the process of change followed.

In the research on community capitals, social capital has received a great deal of attention in the literature. On the other hand, as a community capital, human capital has not been addressed very frequently. This article focuses on how CLDE programs contribute to human capital improvements for individual program participants that result in contributions to the seven capitals at the community level. This can be documented by looking at how participants choose to apply what they learned from the CLDE programs for the benefit of the community, especially in ways that contribute to human and social capital improvements and to a lesser extent the other five capitals.

The research presented here documents how CLDE programs increase the capacity of individuals as leaders as evidenced by improvements in six CLDE program outcome variables. These are (1) personal growth and efficacy, (2) community commitment, (3) shared future and purpose, (4) community knowledge, (5) civic engagement, and (6) social cohesion. (For descriptions of the indices, see the Appendix.) Significant positive improvements in these characteristics should translate into individual engagement and contributions to community projects and activities that build human and social capital within the community. CLDE programs accomplish these outcomes by improving individual leadership skills, increasing the individual's knowledge of the community, and enhancing the individual's social networks. This increases the human capital from an individual perspective and the aggregate human and social capital improvements for program participants contributes to human capital and social capital improvements for communities. To make these connections, leadership program participants are tracked as they participate in community projects that directly and indirectly contribute to human and social capital improvements as well as improvements to the other five capitals. The improvements are manifested through activities such as securing funds for program interventions, serving in various decision-making roles with government and non-profit organizations, and volunteering in the community.

Connecting civic engagement to human and social capital

In his study of democracy in Italy, Putnam (1993) characterizes the civic community as a dense horizontal network of associations where citizens pursue their self-interest within a framework of the broader public interest. It is in these community-based horizontal networks of association that make up the local civil society where community residents build their public discourses and pursue public action (Armony, 2004, pp. 22–23). Community-level social capital is also developed and enhanced, emerging from the broad networks of trust and reciprocity which expand in the civic actions of individuals working together (Putnam, 2000).

It is in this broader framework of public interest where CLDE can have an impact. If, as Putnam (1993, 1995) suggests, civic activity builds interpersonal trust, then we can create additional social capital at both individual and community levels through participation in community affairs (Armony, 2004). Morton (2003) addresses this relationship between the individual and her community in a study of social networks and civic structure. To clarify the distinction between individual-level and community-level social capital, she uses the term civic structure to represent the community-level networks of trust and reciprocity arguing this term better describes the "weak ties" or "bridging forms of social capital" that exist in public domains. Morton also references the distinction made by Stolle and Rochon (1998) who examined the role of associations in community life and noted that "groups and associations may produce high levels of personalized social capital but fail to produce public social capital" (p. 49). Morton (2003) argues that "public social capital is the transition point from micro to macro scale, from personal networks to community-wide networks. ... It is the action/inaction of multiple citizens and groups that create community norms of trust and a macro structure characterized by some degree of high to low expectations of community benefit" (p. 104). This argument parallels that of Orum and Gramlich (1999) although they use the term "civic infrastructure" to denote the public form of social capital.

Armony (2004) cautions that the relationship between civic engagement and democracy in a civil society cannot be properly addressed without considering the patterns of social exclusion (p. 63). CLDE works to address and disrupt these patterns of social exclusion by providing participants with opportunities for human capital improvements which in turn, offers them additional confidence to engage in civic activity thus breaking down perceived or real barriers of social exclusion. In the case of CLDE programs, community residents who are historically not engaged in roles as community leaders are afforded opportunities to become involved in these roles and contribute to the decision-making processes regarding how community resources are developed, amassed, and spent on various community capital building activities. By providing opportunities for human and social capital growth and improvement, individuals can enter into community-based networks of association and strengthen their connections with others, resulting in stronger social capital for the community as a whole. This in turn results in more diverse public discourse, increased social cohesion, and public action that benefit the well-being of the broader community.

For a rural community, understanding the community-level context is critical for creating the situation where effective and positive civic engagement can occur. Rural communities have been experiencing decline, and many have been left behind as society is increasingly urbanizing. This scenario creates the current reality of the broader political and economic factors where government representation and resources at the state and federal levels are increasingly controlled by suburban and urban legislators. To initiate locality-(community) based initiatives in the rural community, it is necessary to augment the ability of local actors to be effective in social interaction and ultimately engage in politically effective civic engagement to create the opportunities for change. This can occur either through successfully arguing for and receiving resources from the larger resource institutions controlled by federal and state governments and suburban and urban dominated legislatures or by effectively engaging local social and political actors in locality-supported initiatives that address community-specific conditions. CLDE programs create the awareness of and the encouragement for civic engagement that results from strengthening individual human capital and social capital.

Community capitals and measuring individual and community effects

The primary challenge for the research presented here is to determine whether the CLDE programs focusing on individual effects lead to community effects. What role do CLDE program interventions play? These programs create the capacity for and empower individuals to engage in civic behavior as leaders. This capacity is demonstrated with six CLDE program outcome variables (presented above) that reflect characteristics or attributes of individuals that may result from participation in CLDE programs. These attributes are inter-related and sequenced together they tend to influence one of them, especially that being "civic engagement."

Phase I research: measuring CLDE program effects on individuals

Six states were selected for study primarily on a convenience basis. Each of the three researchers had prior relationships with colleagues in at least two of the states involved and those relationships were deemed important in conducting of the research. These relationships provided useful insights and sources of information about leadership program activities and participants in each state helping the research team to have to individuals and information more easily. The six states included: Missouri, South Carolina, Illinois, West Virginia, Ohio, and Minnesota.

These six states also use different approaches to their CLDE activities. For example, Missouri had consistently used two approaches; one of these was EXCEL (Cook, 1985) developed by Cooperative Extension, while the other was the typical Chamber of Commerce program for developing community leaders. Illinois also featured the Chamber model along with a Cooperative Extension model that had sometimes been implemented on a multi-county basis. Ohio's leadership programs were sponsored by Chambers, Extension, and universities and Chamber/Extension combined. Both Minnesota and West Virginia featured multiple approaches sponsored by Chambers, Extension, foundations, and other organizations with an interest in leadership development. South Carolina had historically used the Chamber model along with a multitude of approaches used by Cooperative Extension. All states had active programs since at least the year 2000, with some more actively involved than others (i.e. more locations were involved in offering programs).

Sites[1] were chosen within each state that had CLDE programs in place from 2000 to 2006. Once study sites had been selected, the sponsors were asked to provide a list of participants in all the CLDE programs held between 2000 and 2006 along with contact information including email addresses. To demonstrate the effects of leadership development programs, a balanced group of 12 comparison localities was also selected. For the comparison sites, there were no participant lists available so a snowball procedure was used to identify "community leaders." Three individuals were contacted in each site – the Cooperative Extension Agent for that location, the mayor or city/county administrator, and a Chamber or other economic development organization representative – and asked to identify three individuals each that they considered as community leaders. In turn, each of these nine individuals was contacted and similar referrals were requested. These individuals, now numbering as many as 27, were considered the individuals to be invited to participate in the survey after duplicate names were eliminated and email contact information was verified.

In early 2008, an online survey was conducted to determine the effects of participation in community-based leadership development education programs (CLDE) in six states and 24 sites. The online survey also went to the 12 comparison sites (two in each of the six states) where no leadership program was offered. Mail surveys were sent to participants and members of the comparison sites without email addresses. Procedures advocated by Dillman (2007) were followed for both internet and mailed surveys. In the treatment counties, 637 people responded to this online survey with an overall response rate of 62%; in some cases, a smaller number of respondents is reported due to missing data. In the comparison counties, surveys were sent to 240 individuals. Responses were received from 146 individuals, a response rate of 61%. Socio-demographic information on respondents is provided in Table 1.

Table 1.   Socio-demographic characteristics of respondents.

Variable	Treatment counties			Comparison counties		
	Frequency	Percentage	Mean	Frequency	Percentage	Mean
Education						
Less than college degree	176	34.1		48	31.6	
College and above degree	340	65.9		104	68.4	
Sex						
Female	344	66.7		53	34.6	
Male	172	33.3		100	65.4	
Income						
<$100,000.00	350	68.5		88	59.1	
>$100,000.00	115	22.5		48	32.2	
Marital status						
Married	417	81		133	86.9	
Not married	98	19		20	13.1	
Employment						
Employed	462	89.8		118	78.7	
Not employed	53	10.2		32	21.3	
Year living in the community			24.2			30.3
Age			45.6			

The average ages of the respondents in the study were 45.6 and 50.7 years for treatment and comparison groups, respectively. The mean number of years of living in the community for leadership program participants was 24, and for the comparison group it was 30. About 67% of respondents in the treatment group and 35% of the respondents in the comparison group were female. Overall, respondents in the study were well-educated. Approximately 66% of respondents in the treatment group and 68% of respondents in the comparison group had completed college and post-college levels of education. Slightly more than four in five (81% and 87%) of the respondents were married in the treatment and comparison groups, respectively. Most respondents in the study were employed full-time (90% for the treatment group and 79% for the comparison group). About 23% of treatment group respondents and 32% of comparison group respondents reported earning more than $100,000 in annual income.

We used a research methodology that relied upon previously developed instrumentation that had proven reliable in several applications (Pigg, 2000). The measurement technique employed a discrepancy analysis (Provus, 1971) in that participants were asked to rate themselves on the same questions twice, representing the way they assessed their knowledge and skills prior to the educational program, and after this experience was complete. For the comparison locations, the same approach was used except the framework was shifted to reflect a time "five years ago" vs. "today." From these data, the pre-program scores were subtracted from the post-program scores and "outcome" scores were computed. In addition, the individual indicators were organized into six indices, based on previous study, to summarize the impacts experienced. Reliability coefficients were computed for each index and all produced coefficients of about 0.80 (α), meaning these are very reliable indices for use in different settings. For use in this analysis of community effects, the research team aggregated the individual outcome scores on each index and computed an index mean for each location.

Impact scores demonstrate efficacy of leadership development education

As shown in Tables 2 and 3, there are significant differences between the scores on the six outcome indices between the treatment and comparison counties. Table 2 shows the raw scores, for example, index of personal growth and efficacy has a

Table 2. Averages for treatment and comparison counties*.

Outcome indices	Treatment counties			Comparison counties		
	Pre-program	Post-program	N	Five-years ago	Present	N
Personal growth and efficacy	17.1355	20.0120	502	18.7219	20.5828	151
Community commitment	18.0278	21.3241	503	20.5260	22.5325	154
Shared future and purpose	10.4724	12.6713	508	11.9744	13.2179	156
Community knowledge	12.1542	15.4783	506	14.1806	16.1871	155
Civic engagement	13.0059	16.0611	507	15.1364	17.1429	154
Social cohesion	17.3281	19.8103	506	18.5461	20.2500	152

Note: *Mean values of the post-program and the pre-program for treatment counties and mean values of present and five-years ago for comparison counties.

Table 3. Paired mean analysis for six dimensions of community leadership.

	Treatment counties			Comparison counties		
Outcome indices	Mean differences b/w the post- and the pre-program	N	Significant (two-tailed)	Mean differences b/w now and five-years ago	N	Significant (two-tailed)
Personal growth and efficacy	2.87649*	502**	0.000***	1.86093	151	0.000
Community commitment	3.29622	503	0.000	2.00649	154	0.000
Shared future and purpose	2.19882	508	0.000	1.24359	156	0.000
Community knowledge	3.32411	506	0.000	2.00645	155	0.000
Civic engagement	3.05523	507	0.000	2.00649	154	0.000
Social cohesion	2.48221	506	0.000	1.70395	152	0.000

Notes: *2.87649 is the difference between the mean of the post-personal growth index (20.0120) and the pre-personal growth index (17.1355). Mean differences between the post-leadership program and the pre-leadership program is the impact score. **502 is the total number of cases that contributed to the paired mean analysis for the personal growth dimension. ***A low-significance value for the t-test (typically less than 0.05) indicates that there is a significant difference between the two indices, the post and the pre, for the treatment counties and the comparison counties.

pre-program score of 17.14 and a post-program score of 20.01 for an impact (outcome) score of 2.88 which is statistically significant (Table 3). Similar results can be found by examining the remaining results in these two tables. The differences in scores for the treatment county participants and the comparison county participants in the survey were significantly different demonstrating the effect of the treatment (educational program). Interestingly, in all cases the respondents in the comparison counties rated themselves higher in the present and higher in the past in absolute terms than did participants in the treatment counties even though the actual differences were not as large for respondents in the comparison counties. This finding suggests that some learning took place just based on experience in the comparison county group, but a larger amount of learning occurred with those in treatment counties who participated in the educational programs.

Those who participated in leadership programs are assumed to have done so either to become leaders or to improve their leadership skills. Thus, they have individual goals to accomplish which motivated their decision to participate. Based on the results, the programs were effective in helping them achieve these goals as shown by the greater increases in their impact scores compared to those in the comparison counties. Participation in a community-based CLDE program makes a difference in the creation and expansion of the capacity of participants in important outcomes related to leader development. As noted, these outcomes include: civic engagement, social cohesion, personal efficacy, community knowledge and commitment, and shared vision and purpose. Further, the increased capacity in these areas has been demonstrated to be statistically significant.

Socio-demographic variables such as gender, education, income, and years living in the community seem to play important roles in determining whether the study participants benefited and increased their leadership capacities through participation in the community leadership education programs (Table 4). Females in community leadership education programs had significantly greater improvements in their leadership outcome indices than male participants. This occurred for three of the outcome indices: personal growth and efficacy, community knowledge, and civic engagement. Participants without a college degree had significantly higher increases in their leadership skills for the outcome indices of personal growth and efficacy, community commitment, shared future and purpose, and social cohesion. Similarly, leadership education program participants whose incomes were less than $100,000 showed significantly greater improvements in the community knowledge index than those whose annual incomes were above $100,000. Finally, participants who had lived in the community for a shorter period of time had significantly higher increases in the community commitment, shared future and purpose, community knowledge, and civic engagement indices than those who had lived in the community for a longer period of time.

Phase II research: community effects of CLDE participation

Phase II of the research involved collecting information on community projects and activities in the treatment communities. Members of the research team traveled to four localities in each of five states (Phase II was not completed in one state due to logistics and timing) and assembled a focus group of 5–10 key informants who were identified with the assistance of program sponsors. Researchers conducted the focus group interviews to identify community activities and projects implemented from

Table 4. Demographic characteristics and community leadership outcome indices.

Independent variables	Dependent variables					
	Personal growth and efficacy	Community commitment	Shared future and purpose	Community knowledge	Civic engagement	Social cohesion
College and beyond	−0.92*	−0.85*	−0.37*	−0.16	−0.39	−0.67*
Female	0.63*	0.35	0.3	0.26*	0.62*	0.17
Age	−0.01	0	0	0.02	0	−0.02
Marital status	−0.03	0.52	0.08	0.38	0.24	0.17
Employment	−0.38	−0.62	−0.55	−0.59	−0.49	−0.65
Income >$100,000	−0.48	−0.62	−0.15	−0.73*	−0.37	−0.45
Years in living in community	0.01	−0.04***	−0.02*	−0.04***	−0.03***	−0.01
Constant	4.01	4.85	3.22	3.73	3.91	4.44
Changed R^2	0.04	0.05	0.03	0.05	0.02	0.03
ANOVA significant F	0.02	0.01	0.15	0.01	0.03	0.09

Notes: *Significant at 0.01. **Significant at 0.001. ***Significant at 0.000 levels.

2000 to 2009. Information was obtained on each project as well as the names of individuals involved as project leaders. Following the focus group sessions, researchers compared the list of project leaders named by key informants with the individuals in the survey respondent population. Those projects in which the leaders could be identified as CLDE program participants became the focus of further investigation.

Follow up interviews with these identified individuals were conducted by telephone to confirm their involvement in the leadership development program and to discuss their roles in the identified activity(s) or project(s). These project leaders were asked to provide a brief description of the goals and objectives of the project. Each telephone interview with these community project leaders was recorded or extensive notes were taken. Once a relatively complete description of each project or activity was obtained, researchers completed a community capitals checklist (adapted from Magis, 2008). Items on the CCF checklist were reviewed and those present were checked off. The individual project checklists allowed determination of which community capital(s) was the primary capital and which ones were secondary. The checklist enabled the researchers to identify what benefits resulting from the individual activity or project. For example, if a project was designed to raise funds for an educational program or a community park, the primary community capital benefit was financial in nature. Secondary community capital benefits would be human capital for the educational project and social capital for the community park. This qualitative data made it possible to better understand how the community capitals may have been affected as well. If these individuals were participants in a leadership education program before 2000, they were interviewed regarding their involvement in the activity or project as previous study had demonstrated the stability over time of the individual outcome measures being used (Pigg, 2000).

A total of 203 projects were included in the Phase II analysis. For each project, a primary community capital was identified, followed by additional secondary community capitals impacted by the project. Table 5 shows that 58 (28.6%) of the community projects had a primary community capital impact on human capital in the community, followed by 38 (18.7%) projects with a primary community capital impact on financial capital. Primary community cultural capital impacts were attributed to 33 (16.3%) projects, followed by 24 (11.8%) projects that primarily impacted community social capital. Table 5 shows that for the 199 projects where a secondary community capital contribution was identified, 68 (34.1%) projects had an impact on community social capital. Additional secondary community capital impacts included financial capital (44 projects or 22.1%), political capital (35 projects or 17.6%), and human capital (21 projects or 10.6%). A total of 140 projects had a second related community capital contribution with impacts on social capital (50 projects or 35.7%), financial capital (29 projects or 20.7%), political capital (26 projects or 18.6%), and human capital (19 projects or 13.6%). When counting all of the community capital contributions associated with each project, social capital impacts were associated with 154 projects (26.2%) followed by 118 projects with financial capital impacts (20.2%), 105 projects with human capital impacts (17.9%), and 77 projects with political capital impacts (13.1%).

Table 6 shows the number of projects associated with each type of leadership program sponsor, and the distribution of the community capital impacts associated with the projects. Participants in the five Extension sponsored CLDE programs worked on 68 projects. Participants in the six Chamber of Commerce sponsored

Table 5. Primary and secondary community capital impacts for community projects*.

Type of capital	Primary community capital impact		Secondary community capital impact 1		Secondary community capital impact 2		Secondary community capital impact 3		Total	
	Frequency	Percentage	Frequency	Percentage	Frequency	Percentage	Frequency	Percentage	Frequency	Percentage
Social capital	24	11.8	68	34.1	50	35.7	12	26.1	154	26.2
Financial capital	38	18.7	44	22.1	29	20.7	7	15.2	118	20.2
Human capital	58	28.6	21	10.6	19	13.6	7	15.2	105	17.9
Political capital	7	3.4	35	17.6	26	18.6	9	19.6	77	13.1
Cultural capital	33	16.3	11	5.5	8	5.7	3	6.5	55	9.4
Built capital	21	10.3	12	6.0	3	2.1	6	13.0	42	7.1
Natural capital	22	10.8	8	4.0	5	3.6	2	4.3	37	6.3
Total	203	100	199	100	140	100	46	100	588	100

Note: *There were 203 projects identified in Phase II. Each project was assigned a primary community capital impact. Some projects had one, two, or three secondary community capital impacts.

Table 6. Summary of community capital impacts for projects by program sponsor.

	Extension (68)* (5)**		Chamber of commerce (22)* (6)**		Chamber of commerce and Extension (41)* (3)**		Other*** (72)* (6)**	
	Frequency	Percentage	Frequency	Percentage	Frequency	Percentage	Frequency	Percentage
Natural capital	10	5.6	3	4.4	2	1.6	17	7.9
Human capital	35	19.4	10	14.9	23	18.7	37	17.1
Cultural capital	20	11.1	7	10.5	13	10.6	15	6.9
Built capital	11	6.1	7	10.5	8	6.5	18	8.3
Financial capital	38	21.1	17	25.4	26	21.1	38	17.6
Social capital	46	25.6	15	22.4	35	28.5	58	26.9
Political capital	20	11.1	8	11.9	16	13	33	15.3
Total	180	100	67	100	123	100	216	100

Notes: *Number of projects. **Number of programs. ***Other sponsors include non-profits, foundations, city councils, development associations, and school boards.

CLDE programs were involved in 22 projects. For the three programs jointly sponsored by the Chamber of Commerce and Extension, participants worked on 41 projects. Participants in the six "Other" sponsored CLDE programs were involved in 72 projects and the distribution of the community capital impacts were similar to the total community capital impacts (Table 5). Community social capital impacts are attributed to 28.5% of the projects associated with programs sponsored by the Chamber of Commerce and Extension together, followed by 26.9% for projects associated with other sponsored programs, 25.6% for projects associated with Extension sponsored programs, and 22.4% of projects associated with Chamber of Commerce sponsored programs. Financial capital impacts were the highest for the Chamber of Commerce sponsored programs (25.4%) and were second highest for the other three types of sponsored programs. Human capital impacts were the third highest for all sponsor types.

Summary and conclusions

The research presented above has several limitations. It was not possible to establish a statistical connection between Phase I and Phase II of the research, since individual-level measures and community-level measures are not comparable. An analysis of the impact of sponsorship on individual outcomes was not included in Phase I of the research reported. There are important questions related to program content and design to be considered in a more detailed analysis that consider individual level differences due to sponsorship. Sponsorship was examined in Phase II using frequency counts and patterns were observed that were similar for all sponsor types.

From a practitioner standpoint, several findings reported above are especially instructive. The development of individual skills and knowledge contribute to human capital improvements for CLDE program participants. In turn, these benefits prepare participants to expand their social networks and take on leadership roles resulting in increases in one or more of the seven community capitals. The CLDE programs in this study all contributed to leader development through documented impacts on the human and social capital of participants as manifest by significant improvements in all six outcome indices. The analysis of the programs above indicates differential benefits for females, those earning less than $100,000 in income, those without a college degree, and those living in the community a shorter period of time. Participants in these groups all benefited more from participation in CLDE programs. Therefore, leader development efforts that target individuals in these groups help to build their human capital potential and prepare them to more fully engage in leadership development in the community. This follows the distinction between leader development and leadership development made by Day (2001) and other (Rasmussen et al., 2011). Leader development builds human capital among individuals and leadership development results when individuals use their human capital potential to build both bonding and bridging social capital.

The individual leaves the CLDE program with increases in personal skill and efficacy, community knowledge, and a better understanding of a shared sense of the future, community commitment, social cohesion, and civic engagement (social and human capital benefits). All of these translate into an improved understanding and knowledge of how to recognize and engage assets in the community. These benefits are carried forward into community development activities as shown by the numerous activities and projects CLDE program participants contributed to in leaders in their communities. While all of the community capitals were represented in the activities and projects identified in this study, it is important to note the four capitals most impacted were human, social, financial, and political. These four capitals represent important contributions to community capacity building. By empowering community residents to become civically engaged in strengthening these community capitals, CLDE programs provide the connecting link between individual attributes and the immediate program effects on individuals and the subsequent effects on communities. In other words, the empirical evidence suggests that CLDE programs help to create the kinds of self-efficacy and the social connections that hold communities together and maintain community quality of life in the face of the challenges facing small and rural communities in the twenty-first century.

Acknowledgment

This material is based upon work supported by the Cooperative State Research, Education, and Extension Service, US Department of Agriculture, under Award No. 2006-35401-17560.

Note

1. "Sites" is the term used here to designate community-level efforts even though the unit of analysis was actually the county. This is justified as many community-based CLDE programs are open to residents throughout an entire county.

References

Armony, A.C. (2004). *The dubious link: Civic engagement and democratization.* Stanford, CA: Stanford University Press.

Black, A.M., & Earnest, G.W. (2009). Measuring the outcomes of leadership development programs. *Journal of Leadership and Organizational Studies, 16,* 184–196.

Block, P. (2008). *Community: The structure of belonging.* San Francisco, CA: Berrett-Koehler Publishers.

Brown, D.L., & Schafft, K.A. (2011). *Rural people and communities in the 21st century: Resilience and transformation.* Cambridge, UK: Polity Press.

Brundgardt, C.L., & Seibel, N. (1995). *Assessing the effectiveness of community leadership programs.* Hutchinson, KS: Kansas Leadership Forum Publication Series.

Cook, J.B. (1985). *EXCEL: Experiment in community leadership.* Columbia, MO: University of Missouri Extension.

Day, D.V. (2001). Leadership development: A review in context. *Leadership Quarterly, 11,* 581–613.

Dhanakumar, V.G., Rossing, B., & Campbell, R. (1996). An evaluation of the Wisconsin rural leaders perspective program. *Journal of Extension, 34.* Retrieved from http://www.joe.org/joe/1996june/rb3.html

Dillman, D.A. (2007). *Mail and internet surveys: The tailored design method.* Hoboken, NJ: John Wiley & Sons.

Earnest, G.W. (1996). Evaluating community leadership programs. *Journal of Extension, 34*(1). Retrieved from http//joe.org/joe/1996february/rbl.php

Emery, M., Fernandez, E., Gutierrez-Montes, I., & Flora, C.B. (2007). Leadership as community capacity building: A study on the impact of leadership development training on community. *Journal of the Community Development Society, 38,* 60–70.

Emery, M., Fey, S., & Flora, C. (2006). Using community capitals to develop assets for positive community change. *CD Practice.* Retrieved from http://www.comm-dev.org/index.php?option=com_content&view=article&id=70&%20Itemid = 81

Emery, M., & Flora, C.B. (2006). Spiraling up: Mapping community transformation with community capitals framework. *Journal of the Community Development Society, 37*(1), 19–35.

Flora, C.B., & Flora, J. 2008. *Rural communities: Legacies and change* (3rd ed.). Boulder, CO: Westview Press.

Green, G.P., & Haines, A. (2007). *Asset building & community development*. Thousand Oaks, CA: Sage Publications.

Hyman, J.B. (2002). Exploring social capital and civic engagement to create a framework for community building. *Applied Development Science, 6*, 196–202.

Langone, C.A. (1992). Building community leadership. *Journal of Extension, 30*. Retrieved from http://www.joe.org/joe/1992winter'a7.php/

Magis, K. (2008). Community resilience measurement protocol: A system to measure the resilience of forest-based communities, partner report. *2010 National report on sustainable forests*. Washington, DC: United States Department of Agriculture, Forest Service.

Morton, L.W. (2003). Small town services and facilities: The influence of social networks and civic structure on perceptions of quality. *City and Community, 2*, 101–120.

Orum, A.M., & Gramlich, J. (1999). Civic capital and the construction and reconstruction of cities. *Colloqui, 14*, 45–54.

Pigg, K.E. (1990). Accountability in community development. *Journal of the Community Development Society, 21*(1), 19–32.

Pigg, K.E. (2000). Community leadership and community theory: A practical synthesis. *Journal of the Community Development Society, 30*, 196–212.

Pigg, K.E. (2001). *EXCEL: Experience in community enterprise and leadership*. University of Missouri, Columbia, MO: University Extension and Outreach.

Pigg, K.E. (2002). Three faces of empowerment: Expanding the theory of empowerment in community development. *Journal of the Community Development Society, 33*(1), 107–123.

Provus, M.M. (1971). *Discrepancy evaluation for educational program improvement and assessment*. Berkley, CA: McCutchan Publishing Corporation.

Putnam, R.D. (1993). *Making democracy work: Civic traditions in modern Italy*. Princeton, NJ: Princeton University Press.

Putnam, R.D. (1995). Bowling alone: America's declining social capital. *Journal of Democracy, 6*(1), 65–78.

Putnam, R.D. (2000). *Bowling alone: The collapse and revival of America community*. New York, NY: Simon and Shuster.

Rasmussen, C.M., Armstrong, J., & Chazdon, S.A. (2011). Bridging Brown county: Captivating social capital as a means to community change. *Journal of Leadership Education, 10*(1), 63–82.

Rohs, F.R., & Langone, C.A. (1993). Assessing leadership and problem-solving skills and their impacts in the community. *Evaluation Review, 17*(1), 109–115.

Rost, J. (1993). *Leadership for the 21st century*. New York, NY: Praeger.

Saegert, S. (2006). Building civic capacity in urban neighborhoods: An empirically grounded anatomy. *Journal of Urban Affairs, 28*, 275–294.

Schafft, K.A., & Brown, D.L. (2003). Social capital, social networks, and social power. *Social Epistomology, 17*, 329–342.

Sharp, J.S., & Parisi, D.M. (2003). Devolution: Who is responsible for rural America? In D.L. Brown & L.E. Swanson (Eds.), *Challenges for rural America in the twenty-first century* (pp. 353–362). University Park, PA: Penn State University. Rural Studies Series.

Stolle, D., & Rochon, T.R. 1998. Are all associations alike? *American Behavioral Scientist, 42*(1), 47–65.

University of Michigan School of Social Work. (2007). *Leadership development*. Retrieved from http://www.ssw.umich.edu/public/currentProjects/goodheighborhoods/Leadership_Development_Brief.pdf

Wagner, W. (2004). Beyond dollars and cents: Using civic capital to fashion urban improvements. *City and Community, 3*, 157–173.

Whent, L.S., & Leising, J.G. (1992). A twenty-year evaluation of the California agricultural leadership program. *Journal of Agricultural Education, 33*, 32–39.

Appendix. Descriptions of CLDE impact indices

(1) Personal growth and efficacy: The index items used here reflect the sort of skills considered most useful to community leaders and for which there are few other opportunities for learning these skills. As a result, many community residents who may otherwise be motivated to provide leadership and recognize needs for leadership in the community may be reluctant to attempt it, perceiving they lack both skill and confidence (feeling of efficacy). The index includes items that deal with public speaking skills, working with different kinds of groups and needs, problem identification and analysis, consensus building skills, and a commitment to personal growth.

(2) Community knowledge: Community information and knowledge provide an opportunity for community residents to take stock of community assets and to take the necessary steps to exploit them for a community's benefit. A significant contributor to leader effectiveness is knowledge of the community and "how it works," or how decisions get made, what the social and political culture is, where to find resources to support local efforts, local history and behavior norms, and what the local structure of needs may be. Knowing these kinds of things provides community leaders with an ability to act in concert with local norms, to mobilize resources more effectively, and engage influential people in the community who can be of assistance. Community knowledge also relates to the development of an appropriate vision for community success.

(3) Shared future and purpose: Community leaders need to provide residents (whom they hope will be followers) with a compelling vision to support action. The development of such a vision means that leaders and followers will share the same purpose in their action and direct resources mutually toward the same end. Items in this index reflect the importance of being able to communicate a promising future and convincing vision, to seek out new possibilities for development, confidence that the community can be successful and overcome any challenges it may encounter.

(4) Community commitment: Involves applying resources, including time and money, to improve the quality of life in the community, and make it a better place for everyone. Commitment includes the idea that community leaders take the responsibility to spearhead community activities and work to promote a respectful and inclusive workplace for all including minorities, people with physical disabilities, and those with different sexual orientations. Community leaders' involvement in various local activities is evidence of commitment and feelings of ownership and pride in the local community. Items in this index reflect various dimensions of this commitment such as having a sense of ownership for what happens in the community and belonging to the community itself, being involved, working to improve the community and an appreciation for local business, and other social and economic infrastructure.

(5) Civic engagement: Commitment of leaders is usually best reflected in their involvement in the community. Being engaged in civic affairs means leaders are directly involved in addressing public issues and needs, that they are engaged in significant ways in providing leadership in some fashion even as they strive to extend that leadership into new areas, that leaders have developed trust among some group of followers that provide a base for civic influence, and, further, that leaders have some confidence they can lead in elected positions if appropriate. Civic engagement activity can include community problem solving, volunteering regularly for organizations, participating in fund-raising, maintaining an active membership in a group or association, and supporting other fund-raising for charitable endeavors within a community.

(6) Social cohesion: A cohesive community, one that works together to get things done, is more likely to be successful than a divided community. Divided communities are filled with conflict that acts as an obstacle to success and get in the way of building a consensus to support action. This index examines how leaders think about diversity in their community, the importance of building relationships with others, building a support base among diverse groups, and being willing to listen and respond to the diverse views of different population groups in the community.

Evaluating an asset-based effort to attract and retain young people

William Andresen

UW-Extension, Community Resource Development, USA

The loss of young people is a common issue facing many small towns and rural areas across the United States. Numerous community development strategies have been implemented to attract and retain these young people to help sustain local communities and economies. This paper discusses one such strategy and explores the evaluation methodology used to measure its effectiveness. An asset-based community development initiative aimed at attracting and retaining young people was introduced in northern Wisconsin and the western edge of Michigan's Upper Peninsula in 2008. A survey of the community's young people led to the creation of an asset map for the range. Community residents worked to strengthen, promote, and connect its young people to these mapped assets. A 10-year evaluation plan was created to measure the effectiveness of this community-based initiative. A variety of qualitative and quantitative measurement tools were used to evaluate the resulting short-term changes in learning and mid-term changes in action. The evaluation process identified both programming strengths and weaknesses that could be valuable for other community development professionals working to attract and retain young people in their own rural small towns or communities.

Introduction

The movement of young people away from rural America is not new. Population movements in the United States have been marked by the growth of urban areas at the expense of people moving away from rural areas for decades (Lichter & Brown, 2011). Young, educated people represent the highest rates of out-migration from rural areas (Domina, 2006). Roughly 70% of young, single, and college-educated adults living in non-metropolitan areas reported moving between 1995 and 2000, with 75% of them choosing to live in a different county (US Census Bureau, 2003). The brain drain is especially severe in rural communities with traditional agricultural and manufacturing economies (Goudy, 2002). Chronic employment losses, declining tax bases, and high levels of poverty are only a few factors that lead to places that Cornelia and Jan Flora label "persistent poverty communities" where "Those who can leave do. Those who can't leave simply make do" (Flora & Flora, 2008, p. 21).

Three broad categories of strategies exist to attract and retain youth in rural areas and small towns (Winchester, 2010). First are "on the map" strategies that promote the community through electronic media or other creative approaches such as matching potential workers to vacancies in the community or coordinating with local realtors to track prospective new residents. Second are employment-related strategies such as recruiting telecommuters from larger cities or through business succession planning. Third are support strategies to connect new residents with the social capital of the community through welcome wagons, social networking opportunities, and special events.

Carr and Kefalas (2009) argue that new strategies will be necessary to reduce or reverse the loss of young people in rural communities. "The popular tactic of luring even medium-sized companies to small towns with incentives, tax breaks, and the promise of an eager workforce, a practice often referred to as 'elephant hunting', is ineffective for most small towns. The counterpoint to elephant hunting is often called 'economic gardening' and the focus is on planting multiple seeds for local growth in the hope that some will bear fruit" (Carr and Kefalas, 2009, p. 155).

For example, researchers in the western panhandle of Nebraska demonstrate overall population losses in the region, but gains in the 30–44 years old cohort (Burkhart-Kriesel, Cantrell, Johnson, Narjes, & Vogt, 2007). Rather than viewing rural America entirely through the lens of a brain drain, the researchers believe that the growth in educated, skilled, and slightly older adults is actually a brain gain for their region. They argue that communities and regions should take advantage of the experience, skill sets, and entrepreneurial abilities that these new residents bring with them to sustain and grow their economies.

In the border region of Northern Wisconsin and the western edge of Michigan's Upper Peninsula, community residents worked to attract and retain young people by strengthening, promoting, and connecting its young people to the community's assets. This paper focuses on two important elements related to this community-based effort. First, it explores the evaluation process used to measure the program's effectiveness. Second, it discusses whether or not the effort succeeded in achieving its mission to attract and retain young people. The evaluation methodology and the initiative being measured may benefit community development professionals working to attract and retain youth in rural and small-town communities.

Background

The Gogebic Range of Iron County, Wisconsin and Gogebic County, Michigan (Figure 1) could be classified as a "persistent poverty community". Iron ore was discovered on the Gogebic Range in the late 1800s and the population of the range boomed to a peak of 43,000 people in 1920. When the mines started closing in the 1920s, the population rapidly declined. The population has declined in every decade for the past 90 years. Today, the population of the range is barely over 20,000 people (US Census Bureau, 1900–2010) (Figure 2).

Consequently, the region lost many young people. Both counties are significantly older than their respective states and the nation. According to the American Community Survey's five-year estimates, Iron County had a median age of 48.7 years in 2009 compared with 37.8 years in Wisconsin. Gogebic County's median age was 45.4 years compared with Michigan's in 37.7 years. Only 16.7% of Iron County residents were younger than 18 years compared with 23.6% for Wisconsin. Only

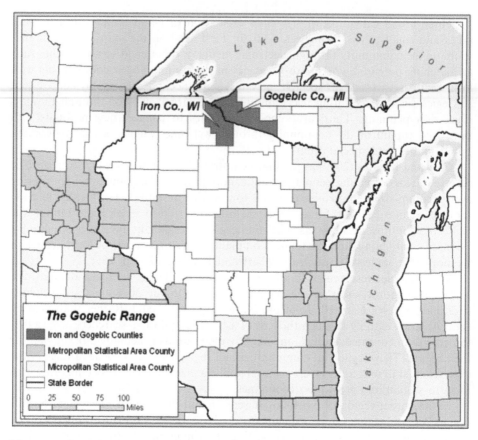

Figure 1.   Gogebic Range location map.

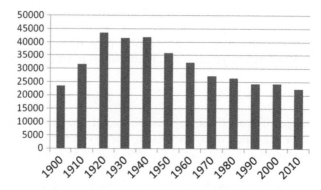

Figure 2.   Gogebic Range population trends (1900–2010). Source: US Census Bureau (1900–2010).

17% of Gogebic County residents were under 18 years compared with 14.3% for Michigan residents. Both counties were significantly older than the nation, which had a median age of 36.5 years with 24.6% of its population under 18 years.

Incomes are also significantly lower on the Gogebic Range, and poverty rates and unemployment rates much higher than the remainder of the two states and the US.

The median household income for Iron County in 2009 was $34,400 compared with $51,569 for Wisconsin and $51,425 for the nation. Gogebic County's median household income was $32,692 compared with $48,700 for Michigan. Poverty rates for residents of Iron County were 14.2% compared with 11.1% for Wisconsin, while Gogebic County's poverty rate was 17.8% compared with 14.5% for Michigan (US Census Bureau, 2010). In June 2011, unemployment rates were 10.7% in Iron County and 12.5% in Gogebic County. This compares with unemployment rates of 8.1% in Wisconsin, 11% in Michigan, and 9.3% for the nation (US Bureau of Labor Statistics, 2011).

Residents of the Gogebic Range conducted an asset-based effort to attract young people understanding that traditional economic development efforts had been largely unsuccessful. Rather than focusing on community weaknesses, asset-based community development focuses on strengthening community assets (Kretzmann & McKnight, 1993). This approach has most recently found favor among many community development professionals. "This focus on the assets of communities, rather than the needs, represents a major shift in how community practitioners have approached their work in recent years" (Green & Haines, 2008, p. 7). The first step in conducting an asset-based community development effort is to identify the community's assets. "Wherever there are effective community development efforts, those efforts are based upon an understanding, or map, of the community's assets, capacities, and abilities" (Kretzmann & McKnight, 1993, p. 5).

To understand what its young people consider to be the community's assets, community leaders in the Gogebic Range conducted a survey of 668 young people in late 2008, including 331 high school juniors and seniors, 205 community college freshmen, and 132 adults in their 20s and 30s. The Michigan Economic Development Corporation conducted the Michigan cool cities survey in 2004, asking 13,500 college students and recent college graduates to rate the importance of 31 location decision-making factors (Michigan Economic Development Corporation [MEDC], 2004). Respondents on the Gogebic Range were asked to rate (on a scale of 1–7, with 1 being low) the importance of the same 31 factors in deciding where to live and to also rate their perception of how well their community offers the same factors.

The survey results were used to create asset maps of the range, displaying the 31 location decision-making factors on both the importance (vertical) and perception (horizontal) dimensions. An asset map displaying the values and perceptions of 50 young adult respondents who moved to the community from someplace else was used to identify the area's most marketable assets, as this group most closely represented the target market (Figure 3).

Factors located in the upper-right quadrant were both important in deciding where to live and perceived as a positive feature of the community. Two categories of assets are clearly evident in the upper-right quadrant of the asset map: "nature-based outdoor recreation" and "core community" assets (Table 1). Rather than addressing unimportant factors or those that are not perceived positively, community leaders focused on the 17 assets that are considered both important and positive.

Community residents worked to strengthen, promote, and connect the community's young people to these mapped assets. The over-arching mission of the efforts was to "attract and retain young people to reverse the decades-long population decline of the Gogebic Range" by the year 2020. More than 100 people were engaged in this asset-based initiative, including community and economic development professionals, local government officials, chamber of commerce

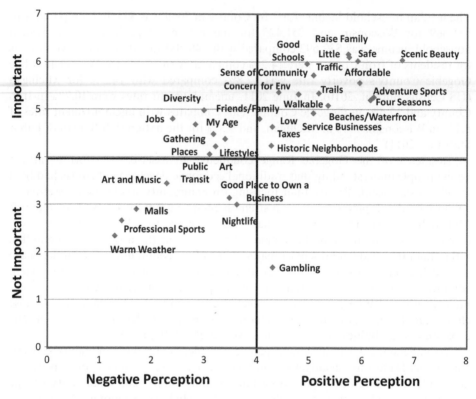

Figure 3.   Gogebic Range asset map.

Table 1.   Gogebic Range assets.

Nature-based outdoor recreation assets	Core community assets
Lots of natural scenic beauty	A place to raise a family
Easy access to adventure sports	Safe streets and neighborhoods
Near trail systems and parks	A place without a lot of traffic congestion
A four-seasons climate	A good public school system
Easy access to beaches or waterfront	An affordable place to live
	A place with a strong sense of community
	Accessible, walkable streets
	A place with a concern for the environment
	A place without high taxes
	Near small service-oriented businesses
	Near where my friends and family live
	Neighborhoods with interesting and unique
	historic or architectural character

representatives, educators, employers, business owners, parents, and interested residents of all ages. The initiative resulted in several new collaborative efforts and positive community development outcomes. The question that this article addresses is whether or not these collaborations and outcomes will result in attracting and/or retaining young people to reverse the population decline.

Evaluation method

The Iron County UW-Extension Community Resource Development educator helped community leaders draft a 10-year evaluation plan to measure the effectiveness of the initiative. Rather than waiting until 2020 to determine if the effort was successful, the evaluation plan listed shorter-term measures that could be used to predict success and guide necessary program modifications.

The evaluation plan included Logic models for each of the initiative's three programming areas of strengthening, promoting, and connecting young people to community assets. Logic models assume that changes in learning can lead to changes in action which can ultimately lead to changes in conditions. These models can be powerful planning and evaluation tools for community change. "Logic models show causal relationships as they relate to one another – a systems approach to portraying the path towards a desired reality" (Millar, Simeone, & Carnevale, 2001, p. 1). On the Gogebic Range, each Logic model listed short-term changes in learning and mid-term changes in action designed to result in the desired long-term outcome of attracting and retaining young people and reversing the community's population decline.

The use of the Logic model approach was deemed especially important in this asset-based community development effort due to strong and long-standing support for traditional economic development strategies aimed at job creation at the expense of asset building and a belief among many residents that the community offered few assets that would be attractive to young people. Therefore, initiative participants agreed that educating residents about the economic benefits of strengthening, promoting, and connecting young people to the community's assets would be a critical step before asking the community to conduct an asset-based effort.

The following sections explore each of the initiative's three programming goals of strengthening, promoting, and connecting young people to the community's assets. Each section displays the short-, mid-, and long-term outcomes listed in each of the Logic models with a description of the methods used to measure their effectiveness, including participant surveys, participant counts, key informant surveys, and observations.

Strengthening local assets

Research supports the efficacy of community development efforts that build on local natural resource assets (Nieto, Schaffner, & Henderson, 1997). "Realizing their advantageous position, knowledge workers choose to reside in amenity-rich areas" (Salvesen & Renski, 2002). Recreational activities offer one amenity resource that is especially effective at attracting and retaining people. In one northern Wisconsin community, 86% of non-resident property owners purchased property for the presence of nearby recreational activities (including an extensive non-motorized trail system), spending as much as $30 million in the community each year (Berard & Trechter, 2007). The direct economic impact of a regional trail in another northern Wisconsin community was estimated at $3.3 million annually (Kazmierski, Kornmann, Marcouiller, & Prey, 2009).

The initiative worked to strengthen its "nature-based outdoor recreation" assets by collaborating with local units of government to create a mapped vision for a regional non-motorized trail system connecting all five cities on the range. Initiative leaders created a presentation script and a sample resolution of support for the regional trail and presented the trail concept to each municipality along the proposed route. The initiative also made numerous presentations to local schools, chambers of commerce, economic development groups, and service clubs and submitted several press releases to the local media to gain a public understanding of the need to strengthen its "nature-based outdoor recreation" assets and support for the regional trail plan. The short-, mid-, and long-term outcomes included in the Logic model for the effort to strengthen the community's assets are shown in Table 2.

Several methods were used to evaluate whether the short- and mid-term outcomes have been realized. The primary method was an electronic survey distributed via email in 2010 to all 120 participants in the initiative. Fifty-two people responded. Respondents represented a relatively balanced mix: (1) 44% grew up in the area and 48% moved to the community from someplace else; (2) 57% were 40 years and older and 43% were in their 20s and 30s; and (3) 42% represented business, 36% represented government/education/health care, and 22% were retired.

Based on the evaluation process used, the short-term changes in learning have been realized. Two of the mid-term changes in action are in place, including the passage of resolutions of support for the regional trail and incorporation of the trail concept into local community development plans. Early progress indicates a high likelihood that the trail will be financed and developed.

Short-term changes in learning: "Heightened awareness of our nature-based outdoor recreation niche"

According to the 2010 survey, 74% of respondents agreed that because of their participation in the initiative they have a better understanding of the community's "nature-based outdoor recreation" assets and 75% believe that the public has a better understanding of these assets as a result of the initiative's outreach efforts.

Short-term changes in learning: "Better understanding of the benefits of strengthening our niche"

According to the same survey, 83% of respondents agreed that because of their involvement in the initiative they have a better understanding of the economic

Table 2. Logic model outcomes for strengthening its assets.

Short-term changes in learning	Mid-term changes in action	Long-term changes in conditions
Heightened awareness of our nature-based outdoor recreation niche	Resolutions of support for mapped vision	More young people move to the Gogebic Range and stay on the Gogebic Range
Better understanding of the benefits of strengthening our niche	Incorporation of mapped vision into community development plans	Increased number of young people living on the Gogebic Range
	Communities obtain internal and external funding for development of trail system	Reverse decades-long population decline of the Gogebic Range
	Trail is developed, maintained, and promoted	

benefits of strengthening the "nature-based outdoor recreation" assets and 66% believe that the public has a better understanding of their economic benefits because of the initiative's efforts.

Mid-term changes in action: "Resolutions of support for mapped vision"

Every municipality along the proposed trail route formally adopted resolutions of support for the regional trail, including two counties, five cities, and three townships. In addition, three neighboring as well as four chambers of commerce, four school boards, and nine additional community-based organizations adopted the same resolution. Plus, two adjoining cities have passed their own joint resolution of support for a two-city riverside trail system that will connect to the regional trail.

Mid-term changes in action: "Communities obtain internal and external funding for development of trail system"

Largely based on strong support from the community, the Michigan Department of Natural Resources has allocated $500,000 for the cost of acquiring the railroad grade for much of the proposed system. In addition, two cities applied for a total of $848,000 in grant funding to develop trailheads along the proposed regional trail.

Mid-term changes in action: "Trail is developed, maintained, and promoted"

While the trail has yet to be developed, a new "railroad grade technical working group" has been formed. The purpose of this group is to devote additional resources to the detailed process of acquiring the necessary easements for the regional trail.

Promoting local assets

People choose to live in places with scenic beauty and high quality of life factors (McGranahan & Wojan, 2007). These quality of life factors are especially important for people wanting to live in small towns and rural areas (Schuett, Jacob, Lu, & Respess, 2008). According to the Michigan Cool Cities Survey, the top 10 location decision-making factors for respondents wanting to live in a small town or rural area are: (1) scenic beauty, (2) safety, (3) affordability, (4) place to raise a family, (5) good schools, (6) sense of community, (7) little traffic, (8) concern for environment, (9) friends and family, and (10) walkable streets (MEDC, 2004). All 10 of these factors are located in the upper-right quadrant on the Gogebic Range asset map.

The initiative worked to promote these assets to the target market of young people living outside of the community. It collaborated with four area chambers of commerce to create the "Beautiful Northwoods Adventure" website promoting both the "nature-based outdoor recreation" and "core community" assets identified in the asset map. The website is being promoted through bumper stickers, posters, brochures, Facebook, and Twitter. Table 3 shows the outcome statements in the Logic model for this effort to better promote the assets of the community.

The evaluation showed that all three short-term outcomes are in place. The mid-term outcomes have been largely met. The target market has accessed the promotional materials and evidence exists that people have considered moving to the range

Table 3. Logic model outcomes for promoting its assets.

Short-term changes in learning	Mid-term changes in action	Long-term changes in conditions
Heightened awareness of community's strengths	Target market will access website, review related promotional materials and consider moving to the Gogebic Range	More young people move to the Gogebic Range from someplace else
Better understanding of the benefits of promoting our strengths		Increased number of young people living on the Gogebic Range
Greater awareness of marketing tools and resources		Reverse decades-long population decline of the Gogebic Range

after viewing the promotional materials. Several people have also requested additional employment or relocation information from the website.

Short-term changes in learning: "Heightened awareness of community's strengths"

According to the 2010 electronic survey of 52 program participants, 76% agreed that because of their participation they have a better understanding of the "core community" assets of the community and 67% believe that because of the initiative's programming the public has a better understanding of these assets.

Short-term changes in learning: "Better understanding of the benefits of promoting our strengths"

In the 2010 survey, 79% of respondents agreed that because of their participation in the initiative they have a better understanding of the economic benefits of promoting its "core community" assets and 64% believed that the public now has a better understanding of the economic benefits of promoting these assets.

Short-term changes in learning: "Greater awareness of marketing tools and resources"

Six participants most closely involved in creating the community website were asked an additional question in the 2010 survey related to this short-term intended outcome. Four participants agreed that because of their involvement in developing the website, they now have a greater awareness of marketing resources and tools to promote the community, while two were neutral.

Mid-term changes in action: "Target market will access website, review related promotional materials, and consider moving to the Gogebic Range"

According to Google analytics, the "beautiful Northwoods Adventure" website received approximately 4500 hits and 10,000 page views from 631 cities in 27 countries in its first 12 months. The Facebook page designed to promote the website currently has 675 fans. The Twitter account has 16 followers. This indicates that people are accessing the website and reviewing its promotional materials. Through observations and anecdotal information, it is clear that many people who are viewing the site are the target market of young people in their 20s and 30s who are not currently living on the range. To determine if, as a result of viewing the materials, they are more likely to move to the range, a second electronic survey was posted on the Facebook page in early 2011. Thirty-three Facebook fans responded to this survey. Ninety-four percent of the respondents believed that the page is an effective way to promote the range as a great place to live and 55% said it has made them more likely to live (either move to or stay) on the Gogebic Range.

The website included a page devoted to employment-related information and a contact page for employment, relocation, and tourism information requests. To date, 32 people requested employment, relocation, or tourism information from this page. These requests were forwarded to the appropriate chambers of commerce, employment agencies, economic development groups, and employers. Qualitative responses to a key informant survey with individuals representing these organiza- tions demonstrated strong support for this approach and cited specific success stories. One chamber official said "I think we should continue with this service. We have sent out quite a few with people following up with the chamber. I think this has been very helpful". One employment agency official said: "I would strongly suggest that you continue. Sometimes we have been able to find opportunities for these people within a very short time". And a local employer said "We have received resumes and are setting up interviews. Please continue, potential employees viewing the website may be the ones that will make a difference in the future as they are probably people that are most interested in coming to and staying in our area".

Connecting students to its assets

The Gogebic Range survey revealed that only 22% of college students and 30% of high school students planned to live on the Gogebic Range. When asked if they would likely return some day after graduating from college or finding a job, this percentage barely increased. After a review of the literature, it was discovered that little research exists to indicate how communities can increase the likelihood that its students will stay in the community or return some day. One explanation for why so few students on the Gogebic Range plan to live in the community after they graduate can be found in the survey results: High school and college students value and perceive many of the assets located in the upper-right quadrant of the asset map much less favorably than adults in the community.

The initiative collaborated with local educational institutions to improve students' perceptions of the community's assets as a way to encourage them to stay or return to the community some day. The initiative partnered with a local high school to offer service–learning opportunities to connect students with the assets of the community. In one project, high-school students photographed natural features of the community and created display boards to share with their peers and others. In a second project, high school students created an all-day learning experience to teach grade school students about the local assets. The initiative also partnered with the local community college to offer a nature-photography lesson. Table 4 displays the intended outcomes listed in the Logic model for this programming element. The evaluation showed that the intended short-term change in learning has been met to a

Table 4. Logic model outcomes for connecting young people to its assets.

Short-term changes in learning	Mid-term changes in action	Long-term changes in conditions
Better understanding of how we can connect students to the community	Students actively participate in programs that will make them feel more connected to the community	More area students stay on the Gogebic Range or return some day
	Increased collaboration between youth service organizations, schools, and other community groups	Increased number of young people living on the Gogebic Range
		Reverse decades-long population decline of the Gogebic Range

limited degree, considerably less than the changes in learning reported for the first two programming efforts. The mid-term changes in action have also been less positive for this element. Student participants have reported stronger connections to the community, but only one high school has been involved in this effort exposing a minority of local students to the initiative's programming. In addition, virtually no effective community collaborations have been initiated or sustained.

Short-term changes in learning: "Better understanding of how we can connect students to the community"

In the 2010 survey of 52 adult participants, 64% agreed that as a result of their participation they have a better understanding of how to better connect students to the community, but less than half (47%) believed that the public now has a better understanding of how to connect students to the community.

Mid-term changes in action: "Students actively participate in programs that will make them feel more connected to the community"

In 2010, 10 high school students participated in photography classes and prepared nature photography display boards that they presented to 375 elementary students and approximately 100 high school students and community residents at a community open house. According to a qualitative program evaluation, participants believed they are better connected to the assets of the community as a result of their experience: "I discovered the beauty of our community", "I learned that there are many outdoor activities in our community", and "I learned that there is more to our community than just the things we see in town and alongside roads".

In 2011, 15 high school students created an all-day service learning experience for 138 second and third grade students. The program included presentations on the great variety of outdoor recreational activities available in the community. Twelve high school students completed an evaluation following their service learning experience. Ten of the 12 said their perceptions of the community became more positive because of their experience, while two said their perceptions did not change. Eight said their experience made them more appreciative of living in the community, while three said it did not make them more appreciative, and one was unsure. One respondent said "I learned that there are a lot of things that we should appreciate more in our area and take less things for granted".

The local community college conducted a nature-photography lesson for its students and the community at large. Four people participated in this event, including three non-traditional college students and one local resident.

Mid-term changes in action: "Increased collaboration between youth service organizations, schools, and other community groups"

Collaboration occurred between UW-Extension staff and one local high school and the community college for the service learning and nature-photography projects. However, neither of these efforts has been maintained over time. Initial conversations have been held with local youth service organizations about various ways to connect students to the assets of the community, but no collaborative efforts have resulted from these discussions to date.

Implications and limitations

It is impossible to predict if this initiative will succeed in attracting and retaining young people and reversing the community's population decline by 2020. However, the Logic model shows that several short- and mid-term outcomes have been achieved to increase the likelihood of realizing the desired long-term outcome.

For example, an enhanced understanding of the community's assets and the importance of strengthening these assets helped the initiative gain the necessary political and community support for the proposed trail system. Resolutions of support were adopted by every municipality, chamber of commerce, and school board along the proposed trail route. This led the Michigan Department of Natural Resources to allocate $500,000 for land acquisition and encouraged local residents to create a committee to coordinate the land acquisition process.

Another example is improved perceptions of the community's assets which led to a collaborative effort to create a community-wide website to promote area assets to the target market of young people living outside of the community. The website and related promotional materials led to more people exposed to community assets and who are now considering moving to the range. In addition, the community now has structural support from employment agencies and chambers of commerce for responding to employment and relocation requests received from the website.

Without the short-term changes in learning (i.e. improved understanding and appreciation of the community's assets), the motivation to mobilize limited community resources may not have been sufficient to achieve the mid-term changes in action that have transpired. And it is more likely that these mid-term changes in action will succeed in achieving the long-term outcomes of attracting and retaining young people to reverse the community's long-term population decline.

One benefit from conducting an evaluation using short- and mid-term outcomes is identifying program elements that are not successful so that appropriate action can be taken in a timely fashion. For example, it is clear that participants struggled with how to connect local students to the assets of the community. Only one of five high schools participated in this effort, the community college program was poorly attended, the effort received little interest from the broader community, and internal leadership in this programming effort is lacking. To be more effective, initiative leaders must better explain the importance of connecting students to the assets of the community, to key stakeholders, and the public.

A real or perceived limitation to this evaluation effort is that the author was closely engaged in both the initiative and the evaluation of the initiative's effectiveness. Although evaluation specialists with the University of Wisconsin Extension provided technical assistance on the evaluation plan, the plan's implementation would have been strengthened if it had been conducted by a third party.

Conclusions

The purpose of this article is two-fold. First, it is intended to demonstrate a methodology for evaluating community development programming in a timely and effective manner. Second, it offers evidence about whether the asset-based approach used on the Gogebic Range is successful in attracting and retaining young people. This knowledge may be useful to other community development professionals facing similar challenges in their communities.

Early outcome indicators suggest that a heightened understanding of local assets and the economic benefits of these assets (short-term changes in learning) have led to significant momentum toward the development of a regional trail system and an effective internet marketing campaign (mid-term changes in action). Because these mid-term outcomes were selected based on their success in other communities, it is expected that they will succeed in attracting and retaining young people to reverse the community's decades-long population decline (long-term changes in conditions).

This evaluation process determined that the efforts to strengthen and promote the community's assets will likely be effective in attracting and retaining young people because the short-term changes in learning are in place and because a strong body of research suggests that these efforts will succeed. However, the effort to retain students by better connecting them to the community has been determined to be less likely to succeed. This conclusion was reached by noting that the short-term changes in learning were not strong which likely resulted in less community support and involvement. A lack of research suggesting interventions to retain young people also contributed to the struggles faced in this programming element.

Careful consideration should be given to identifying the true assets of a community before embarking on an asset-based community development effort. Understanding what the local young people consider the assets of the community will be most effective in attracting and retaining other young people. An asset-based approach to attract young people based on what older adults in the community believe are the assets may be less likely to succeed. In this effort, the values and perceptions of local young people were used to create an asset map of the community. This asset map largely guided the effort's programming goals and will increase the likelihood of its success.

It is too early to determine if the long-term intended outcomes of this effort will be realized. However, the short-term changes in learning that have transpired and the research-based mid-term changes in action achieved indicate a strong likelihood of success. Conducting an evaluation method such as the one described here provides meaningful feedback. Limited resources can be allocated to promising programs and timely adjustments can be made to those with less promise.

The evaluation methodology and the asset-based community development initiative on the Gogebic Range may prove to be a replicable model for other community development professionals working in small towns and rural communities facing the loss of young people.

Acknowledgments

The author thanks the participants of the local initiative, colleagues, and evaluation specialists with the University of Wisconsin Extension for valuable assistance.

References

Berard, D.A., & Trechter, D.D. (2007). *Non-resident property owners and their impact on sawyer county businesses.* Madison, WI: University of Wisconsin Extension.

Burkhart-Kriesel, C.A., Cantrell, R.L., Johnson, B.B., Narjes, C., & Vogt, R.J. (2007). *Newcomers to the Nebraska panhandle: Who are they?* Lincoln, NE: Center for Applied Rural Innovation.

Carr, P.J., & Kefalas, M.J. (2009). *Hollowing out the middle: The rural brain drain and what it means for America.* Boston, MA: Beacon Press.

Domina, T. (2006). Brain drain and brain gain: Rising educational segregation in the United States, 1940–2000. *City and Community, 5,* 387–407.

Flora, B., & Flora, J.L. (2008). *Rural communities: Legacy and change.* Boulder, CO: Westview Press.

Goudy, W. (2002). Population change in the Midwest: Nonmetro population growth lags metro increase. *Rural America, 17,* 21–29.

Green, G.P., & Haines, A. (2008). *Asset building and community development* (2nd ed.). Thousand Oaks, CA: Sage Publications.

Kazmierski, B., Kornmann, M., Marcouiller, D., & Prey, J. (2009). *Trails and their gateway communities: A case study of recreational use compatibility and economic impacts.* Madison, WI: University of Wisconsin Extension.

Kretzmann, J.P., & McKnight, J.L. (1993). *Building communities from the inside out: A path toward finding and mobilizing a community's assets.* Skokie, IL: ACTA Publications.

Lichter, D.T., & Brown, D.L. (2011). Rural America in an urban society: Changing spatial and social boundaries. *Annual Review of Sociology, 37,* 565–592.

McGranahan, D.A., & Wojan, T.R. (2007). Recasting the creative class to examine growth processes in rural and urban counties. *Regional Studies, 41,* 197–216.

Michigan Economic Development Corporation. (2004). *Michigan cool cities survey: Summary of findings.* Lansing, MI: State of Michigan.

Millar, A., Simeone, R.S., & Carnevale, J.T. (2001). Logic models: A systems tool for performance management. *Evaluation and Program Planning, 24,* 73–81.

Nieto, R.D., Schaffner, D., & Henderson, J.L. (1997). Examining community needs through a capacity assessment. *Journal of Extension, 35*(3) Article 3FEA1. Retrieved from http://www.joe.org/joe/1997june/a1.php

Salvesen, D., & Renski, H. (2002). *The importance of quality of life in the location decisions of new economy firms.* Chapel Hill, NC: University of North Carolina at Chapel Hill.

Schuett, M.A., Jacob, J.S., Lu, J., & Respess, L. (2008). Keeping our charm: Residents, growth, and quality of life issues in a small but growing Texas coastal community. *Journal of Extension, 46*(6) Article 6FEA1. Retrieved from http://www.joe.org/joe/2008december/pdf/JOE_v46_6fea1.pdf

US Bureau of Labor Statistics. (2011). *Local area unemployment statistics.* Washington, DC: US Department of Labor.

US Census Bureau. (1900–2010). *Decennial census.* Washington, DC: US Department of Labor.

US Census Bureau. (2003). *Migration of the young, single, and college educated: 1995 to 2000.* Washington, DC: US Department of Labor.

US Census Bureau. (2010). *2005–2009 American community survey 5 year estimates.* Washington, DC: US Department of Labor.

Winchester, B. (2010). *Regional recruitment: Strategies to attract and retain newcomers.* Crookston, MN: The EDA Center.

Engaging youth in community change: three key implementation principles

David Campbell and Nancy Erbstein

Department of Human and Community Development, UC Davis, USA

Youth are an often untapped but potent resource for community change. To engage youth in community change coalitions requires more time, resources, and intentionality than many anticipate, making it imperative to base the work on well-established principles. Using outcome and process data from a multi-year initiative in seven communities, we describe beneficial results for youth, adults, and communities. The analysis of the most successful community-scale action finds that three implementation principles are critical: (1) asking the right strategic questions in the right order; (2) creating organizational structures and processes that integrate youth and adults into joint decision making; and (3) marshaling boundary-spanning community leaders with diverse skills and extensive networks. The research highlights how community development ideas can augment the predominant research emphasis on youth engagement methods and individual developmental outcomes, focusing attention on whether communities have the leadership and institutional capacity to nurture and sustain youth voice in public life.

Introduction

Young people are a powerful – if often untapped – resource in promoting community change that benefits children, youth, and families (Brennan & Barnett, 2009; Ginwright & James, 2002; Pittman, 2000). While public opinion often tends to view youth either as *problems to be solved* or as *passive clients* of community youth programs, an alternative view posits youth as civic assets whose insights and contributions are essential to build healthy communities. What choices do community developers face in pursuing this agenda? What principles should they consider as they pursue youth civic engagement? What strategies, organizational structures, and leadership skills are critical to success?

To answer these questions, this article draws on an evaluation that compared youth civic engagement approaches and outcomes in seven communities funded by the Sierra Health Foundation's REACH youth program (Campbell, Erbstein, Fabionar, Wilcox, & Cruz Carrasco, 2010). The program funded seven coalitions in the greater Sacramento, CA, region to engage youth and adults in planning and implementing community change strategies. Grantees received 9-month planning grants of $75,000; implementation grants of $200,000 per year for 3 years; technical assistance in the areas of youth development, coalition development, policy, and sustainability; and opportunities to apply for supplemental foundation resources. The initial guiding theory of change was the "Community Action Framework for Youth Development" developed by Youth Development Strategies, Inc., which posits a model of systems change to increase developmental supports and opportunities across multiple contexts (e.g., home, school, and neighborhood; Gambone, Klein, & Connell, 2002). The model emphasizes multi-stakeholder coalitions, institutional reform to coordinate youth services, policy changes that impact practice, and realignment of public and private resources to support local objectives. Although it is not a clearly articulated element of this framework, youth engagement was a guiding principle of the foundation program.[1]

Common features across the seven sites included a shared goal of linking meaningful youth engagement to community-scale change, exposure to training and capacity building led by a foundation-funded technical assistance team, and location in the greater Sacramento, CA, region. On the other hand, the seven coalitions varied significantly in their specific locale, median income levels, lead agency characteristics, coalition model or approach, and the chosen focus of their community change activities (Table 1). The ambitious goal of linking youth engagement to community change, the diversity of community settings, and the considerable freedom of grantees to experiment with different strategies and approaches made the initiative a rich but challenging research laboratory. The foundation offered participating communities guiding principles and frameworks but did not specify a specific intervention or community change objective, making it difficult to develop quantifiable comparisons.

In light of this program context and the lack of robust theoretical models of youth participation in community development, the evaluation design treated the seven settings as natural case-study experiments (Glaser & Strauss, 1967; Lincoln & Guba, 1985). Researchers built empirical generalizations from systematic, cross-case analyses of how to engage youth in community change (Zeldin, Petrokubi, & Camino, 2008). The approaches used a community development lens, a departure from the predominant youth development emphasis of most studies. Instead of emphasizing what it takes to engage youth and foster their individual developmental outcomes, the focus here is on the principles and practices that enable local coalitions to achieve successful community outcomes while including youth in meaningful roles.

The next section reviews key ideas and debates in the literature positing the significant promise of youth civic engagement as part of a community development strategy. After introducing the study's research methods, the following section describes the community intervention studied, including: (1) the nature of youth and adult participants, (2) youth engagement approaches and activities, and (3) observable program outcomes at the individual and community levels. The findings and discussion section argues that three emergent implementation principles should guide other communities as they craft youth engagement strategies. The conclusion argues that the insights of community developers are crucial in formulating questions for future research in what is still a relatively new field of inquiry.

Relevant literature on youth civic engagement

Research identifies multiple rationales for engaging youth in community change, including informing local planning and policy with unique youth knowledge and

Table 1. Comparing the seven research settings.

Community	Locale	Median household income*	Lead agency	Coalition form	Focus
El Dorado Hills	Upscale suburb of 30,000	$92,000	Existing community coalition	Hub for collaboration, grant seeking, and re-granting	Drug and alcohol abuse prevention
Galt	Small city of 28,000 and surrounding unincorporated communities	$30–70,000	School district	Activity hub for students from multiple schools	Developing youth master plan, service learning
Meadowview	Large urban neighborhood of 37,000	$29–35,000	Faith-based community organizing network	Community organizing	High school graduation rates, workforce development
Rancho Cordova	Newly incorporated city of 53,000	$46,000	Nonprofit social service agency	After-school youth group tied to preexisting collaborative	Youth safety
South Sacramento	Large urban neighborhood of 73,000	$27–32,000	Mutual Housing Association	Adult and youth committees on priority topics	Youth arts, safety, jobs, mentoring
West Sacramento	Growing city of 40,000	$27–36,000	Nonprofit healthcare provider	Youth group connected to youth/adult coalition	Increase youth voice in governance
Woodland	City of 52,000	$37–47,000	Family Resource Center	Youth group connected to youth/adult coalition	Teen pregnancy prevention, youth advocacy

Note: *Range reflects highest and lowest figures for different zip codes within the coalition's footprint area, based on US Census 2000 data, downloaded September 2006 at http://factfinder.census.gov/home/saff/main.html?_lang=en.

insight; accomplishing community projects with youth energy and labor; building strategic constituencies for community change; and holding decision makers accountable through youth advocacy (Checkoway & Gutierrez, 2006; London, Zimmerman, & Erbstein, 2003). For youth themselves, civic engagement can deepen civic commitment, extend social capital, create meaningful relationships with adults, foster self-esteem and identity development, and build a sense of self and collective efficacy (Gambone, Yu, Lewis-Charp, Sipe, & Lacoe, 2006; Hughes & Curnan, 2000; Irby, Ferber, Pittman, Tolman, & Yohalem, 2001).

Seeking to capitalize on this promise, youth civic engagement has been a research focus of scholars in the areas of adolescent development and democratic participation. Characteristics associated with successful youth civic engagement include viewing youth as assets and resources (Benson, 1997; Ferman, 2005; Lerner & Benson, 2003; Varney, 2007; Watts & Flanagan, 2007; Wheeler & Edlebeck, 2006); fostering youth ownership of the process while providing adequate capacity-building opportunities and adult support (Camino & Zeldin, 2002; Carlson, 2006; Perri, 2007; Varney, 2007; Wheeler & Edlebeck, 2006); inviting youth to participate in public work with real consequences (Boyte, 2004; Flanagan & Levine, 2010; Hildreth, 2000; Nagda, McCoy, & Barrett, 2006); and involving a broad range of youth socializing institutions, organizations, and systems (Benson, 1997). Researchers have also documented a variety of specific vehicles for engaging youth in the community, including community service, youth-produced media, youth philanthropy, action research and evaluation, political activities, community organizing, and youth in governance (Gray & Hayes, 2008; Libby, Sedonaen, & Bliss, 2006; London et al., 2003).

An important segment of the literature argues against universal, one-size-fits-all approaches and in favor of tailoring initiatives to the circumstances of particular disadvantaged, and typically under-represented, youth populations and communities (Balsano, 2005; Flanagan & Levine, 2010; Sanchez-Jankowski, 2002; Sherrod, 2003; Sherrod, Flanagan, & Youniss, 2002; Watts & Flanagan, 2007; Wheeler & Edlebeck, 2006). Some scholars argue that youth civic engagement should embrace a social justice orientation that helps disadvantaged youth (Ginwright & James, 2002; HoSang, 2006a; Libby et al., 2006; Evans & Prilleltensky, 2005). Others share the concern with engaging disadvantaged youth but emphasize the use of multiple civic pathways – including religious organizations, community colleges, the military, and AmeriCorps – to provide civic engagement opportunities that will benefit youth and communities (Flanagan & Levine, 2010).

Relatively little attention has been devoted to how communities organize efforts to integrate youth voice into community-scale change, although there are important exceptions (Carlson, 2006; Christens & Dolan, 2011; Ginwright, Noguera, & Cammarota, 2006; Sirianni, 2005; Zeldin et al., 2008). Many of the practical suggestions scattered throughout the literature emphasize youth development approaches. One approach emphasizes establishing a group where youth can explore new identities and rotate through various roles (Hildreth, 2000; Perri, 2007). Another emphasizes reflection and analysis so youth have space to explore various conceptualizations of themselves and the community work (Hildreth, 2000). Others take advantage of kinship networks to build intergenerational mobilization efforts (HoSang, 2006b). Still another approach frames youth opportunities at multiple levels, from short-term, hands-on community service, to advisory roles on adult-led boards or projects, to shared leadership on significant community initiatives (Carlson, 2006; Wheeler & Edlebeck, 2006).

This research seeks to complement these useful ideas with key strategic considerations developed in the community development and public policy literatures. Of particular importance are well-established ideas about what it takes to build a successful community change coalition, including:

(a) *clarity of purpose and focus*: the ability to articulate overall community-scale change objectives with broad appeal while also establishing concrete priorities that compel the attention of task-specific groups (Gardner, 2005; Stone, Orr, & Worgs, 2006);

(b) *community legitimacy*: broad and inclusive membership that is sustained over time and engages youth voice in meaningful ways (Flora, Sharp, Flora, & Newlon, 1997);

(c) *mobilization of resources*: evidence that existing networks are tapped and expanded, partners are contributing their own resources to the larger effort, and resources are strategically realigned to support coalition goals (Gardner, 2005; Kubisch, 2005);

(d) *policy development*: a strategy targeting particular policies or systems to change and particular constituencies to mobilize (Kubisch, 2005; Stone et al., 2006); and

(e) *institutionalization*: evidence that the work has an organizational home, skilled staff, and decision-making processes that are fair and depersonalize conflict (Flora et al., 1997; Stone et al., 2006).

Research methods

The goal of this analysis is not to statistically compare outcomes or rank the relative efficacy of the various youth engagement methods and approaches used in the seven sites. That work will require a more controlled setting in which issues of validity and reliability can be ascertained with greater confidence. Instead, this research identifies key explanations for the overall pattern of success and failure across the seven cases. Confidence in these explanations is rooted in two factors. First, the research team had regular, repeated, and timely access to the ways in which initiative stakeholders of all types made sense of the initiative in their own thinking (Weick, 1995). Second, the team was immersed in extensive fieldwork, providing multiple and varied opportunities to objectively appraise what was happening and why. By comparing the insights, concerns, and reflections of stakeholders with differing initiative roles, both within and across local settings – and subjecting those to correction from research team perspectives as objective observers – the research pinpointed key lessons learned from the implementation process with a high degree of confidence.

Research team members (including two faculty and three graduate students) were each assigned to cover one or more of the seven community coalitions. During the 3-year period (May 2007–April 2010), data were collected on local processes, outcomes, and contexts, using these methods:

- observations of coalition meetings, special events, and cross-site convenings (320 total);
- multiple waves of interviews (recorded and transcribed) with youth and adult participants (including foundation staff, technical assistance providers, coalition staff and members, local community leaders unaffiliated with the

coalition, and parents of youth participants), beginning in the first year of implementation (346 in all, 87 with youth);

- youth and adult attendance documentation;
- review of documents, including grantee reports to the foundation and newspaper stories;
- youth-produced digital media documenting community issues in need of attention;
- secondary data profiles generated for each locality using US Census data; and
- surveys to document youth experience with community supports and opportunities.

Researchers coded interview transcripts and field observation notes, identifying coalition activities, outcomes, and challenges. Lead researchers for each local area used the coded materials and other data sources to prepare case analysis memos, using common guidelines. Each of the five research team members individually analyzed the full set of case memos to identify themes with respect to coalition development, youth engagement and community change outcomes, and implementation challenges. One strand of the analytical work examined practices associated with strong community-scale outcomes within cases and then looked across change processes. The team then collaboratively integrated individual researchers' analyses into a final set of findings, seeking not only to document what worked well across the settings but why. This process was repeated twice, at the mid- and end-points of the research. To test the validity of our generalizations, researchers invited critique by community, technical assistance, and foundation stakeholders, who commented on draft reports. While more research is needed to test their applicability in other settings, the findings are supported by a consensus among initiative stakeholders and confirming evidence from our dataset.

The nature of the intervention

Youth and adult participants

Based on coalition attendance reports and observations by researchers during meetings, estimates of ongoing participation levels ranged between 12 and 18 youth and between 6 and 10 adults in each community. Over 3 years, more than 500 youth and a nearly equal number of adults were involved. Age distributions varied significantly across coalitions and included students in elementary school (23%), middle school (35%), and high school (42%). While the initiative had targeted 10- to 15-year olds, leaders were happy when they were encouraged to include older youth, who were often better able to understand and contribute to the work of community change. Youth participants were diverse in terms of gender, ethnicity, and, to some extent, socioeconomic status, again with significant variation between coalitions. For example, in only one of the seven localities do White students constitute more than 50% of the public school population; some have sizable populations of three or more ethnic groups (primarily Latino, Southeast Asian, and African-American), while others are predominantly White and Latino. Recruitment strategies varied: in some cases, adults sought out youth thought to have leadership potential, in others they recruited disadvantaged, under-engaged youth.

Adult participants were drawn from a wide range of community sectors and types of organizations. Despite the tendency for some participants to view them as impenetrable bureaucracies, school personnel represented approximately one in four adult coalition members (Fabionar & Campbell, 2010). Other significant public partners included youth commissions, police, parks and recreation, mental health agencies, and transportation departments. In two cases, local faith-related organizations played important roles. As the initiative progressed, organizers began to realize that parents or caretakers were important partners. Subsequently, they reached out with activities to expand (1) social connections and relationships; (2) parent training and education; and (3) direct parental engagement in the coalition and/or with their children's schools. While all parents welcomed opportunities to socialize with other parents and build social connections, engagement proved especially important for parents of low socioeconomic status – especially immigrants and/or non-English speakers. Often disconnected from schools or other community institutions, these parents reported acquiring better understanding of the US educational system and knowledge about community resources that would enable them to better support their children (Cruz Carrasco & Campbell, 2010).

Coalition goals, activities, and approaches

The approaches that organizations used to engage youth included community service/service learning, media and art, philanthropy, research and evaluation, civic engagement, community organizing, and direct involvement in decision making and governance. The examples ranged in significance from one-time only community clean-up projects, to ongoing youth service on community boards or committees, to sustained efforts to organize youth voice in ways that change local institutions or policies (Table 2). While these types of activities have been documented in previous studies (Gray & Hayes, 2008), the unusually rich local data set helped identify three underlying approaches to youth civic engagement that cut across and undergird the more specific strategies. The three approaches have contrasting strengths and limitations, which community developers should take into account as they seek to adapt strategies to their settings, goals, and resources:

(1) *Relational*: This approach prioritizes establishing deep relationships with youth – meeting them where they are, spending significant time with them, listening to their concerns, and discovering their unique gifts and talents. This process builds relationships of trust and loyalty that are a basis for deep and sustained participation in community change efforts, as well as personal growth. However, the approach is time and resource intensive and dependent on adult capacities that are not always present.

(2) *Activity-based*: This approach creates multiple civic engagement opportunities for youth linked to an overarching community change objective, especially short-term, action-oriented projects that do not require sustained participation. This approach does not depend on deep relationships, provides opportunities for greater numbers of youth, and appeals to youth who do not necessarily want to spend considerable time attending meetings. On the other hand, it tends to attract those already inclined to participate and can sometimes be driven primarily by adult interests, since they often shape the activities.

(3) *Agenda-driven*: This approach pursues a community change agenda on its own terms and looks for multiple ways to engage young people in further defining and advancing this agenda. While assuming that youth will benefit

Table 2. Examples of youth civic engagement opportunities created.

Youth service Volunteering, community service, and service learning	• Community clean-up and service projects • Organized event to raise awareness about disabilities • Organized Youth Leadership Conferences for hundreds of youth
Youth media Participation through public art	• Produced and screened five youth-produced documentaries about community conditions[2] • Launched monthly art walk featuring youth-produced art • Painted murals representing city history on building walls
Youth philanthropy Fundraising and grantmaking	• Raised over $20,000 to benefit children in Africa • Gave out mini-grants to support needy students, events, and emergency preparedness • Funded projects on hunger, literacy, and the environment
Youth in research and evaluation Contribution to research design and implementation	• Survey identifies types of programs to be supported by parcel tax • Youth research displayed in comic book increases awareness about unsafe places
Youth in governance Electoral activities, planning participation, and political voice	• Community members/youth inform youth master plan • Youth protest school budget cuts on steps of the state capitol • Sacramento mayoral candidates answer youth questions at debate • Youth share perspectives on school budget cuts with school board • Youth work with architects to inform park design • Youth advisory councils for city and community services district • Juvenile Justice and Delinquency committee reserves seats for two youth representatives
Youth organizing Strategies to create institutional change	• Students mobilize to press for changes in school discipline policies • Youth advocate for tax to fund youth programs

from participation in the change process, this approach prioritizes community outcomes over individual youth outcomes. Youth are offered various ways to be directly involved in significant real world change efforts. On the other hand, this approach potentially exposes youth to situations for which they are unprepared or even places the broader, project purpose ahead of participating youth interests.

Evidence of youth-focused community change outcomes

Community change that promotes youth well-being can be viewed in various ways – as the aggregation of changes to individuals; as improvements to community organizations, networks, or policies; as measurable changes in community-scale indicators; or as an accumulation of changes across these scales. The initiative provided significant benefits to individual adult and youth participants, along with positive changes in youth-serving organizations, institutions, and policies. These benefits included acquiring new knowledge about youth development principles and practices, developing experience with a variety of specific youth civic engagement methods and approaches, and increasing institutional and civic leaders' interest in youth input.

Interview and observational data indicate that a core group of more than 100 youth with sustained high levels of participation gained key developmental capacities, including:

- meaningful relationships with adults within and beyond their coalitions;
- skills in public speaking and in how to organize and lead meetings;
- a heightened sense of civic responsibility;
- knowledge about local systems and policy change strategies;
- greater self-confidence in dealing with peers and adults;
- additional knowledge about college opportunities and career ambitions; and
- new connections with peers in their own and other communities, including those from socioeconomic or racial backgrounds very different than their own.

Broad, community-scale changes do not happen in a single leap but involve small steps that create visible results and build momentum. The seven coalitions produced a number of such promising achievements related to key policy or community development outcomes (Table 3). Accomplishments included shaping more positive public perceptions of youth, embedding youth development and engagement principles within key institutions, informing community planning and design, building social and political capital, generating new investments and resources, and developing new policies. All seven coalitions enhanced community capacity by becoming catalysts for youth-related activity in their respective communities, although they also struggled with one or more key functions, including broadening and retaining membership, mobilizing community resources beyond those provided by the grant or the lead organization, and finding structures and processes that effectively integrate youth and adults into decision making. Overall, stakeholders expressed pride but with some ambivalence about the results: glad for the achievements, but acutely aware that their impact on community-scale indicators or policy reform had fallen short of the relatively high expectations originally accompanying the grant.

Findings and discussion: three key implementation principles

In examining outcome and process data for this study, the hope was to identify factors pivotal in enabling coalitions to produce promising community-scale outcomes. Looking first within each of seven cases and then across the cases, and guided by the insights and reflections of those who played roles in implementing the initiative, the evidence supports the important role played by three implementation principles:

(1) asking (and answering) the right strategic questions in the right order;
(2) creating structures that integrate youth and adults into joint decision making; and
(3) marshaling boundary-spanning community leaders with diverse skills and extensive networks.

Together these principles focus attention not on specific youth engagement methods, but on the degree to which communities have the leadership and

Table 3. Promising steps toward community change.

Shape public perceptions/ agenda setting	• Foster positive media coverage of youth • Focus attention on key youth issues and potential solutions • Focus public on the problems of underage drinking, tobacco, and drug use • Youth inform discussions of teen pregnancy, school budget cuts, etc. • Youth research with university partner leads to recommendations on transportation, community pride, education, and recreation
Embed youth engagement in institutions	• Created a local go-to place for youth development ideas and activities • School superintendent commits to train staff in youth development • Service learning method diffused throughout community • Parks and Recreation Department starts a youth advisory council • New youth council created at a low-income housing development • Revive city youth commission • Build support for school board's student representative to be a voting member
Inform community planning and design	• Community adopts comprehensive youth master plan covering ages 0–24 • Youth voice and perspective help gain new public bus routes • Youth helps design neighborhood park • Collect data and built support for youth safety compact
Build social and political capital	• Increase youth and their parents/caretakers contact with elected officials, agency representatives, and other community leaders • City departments and schools report working more collaboratively • Strengthen community links with local university
Generate new investments and resources	• Secured large and small new grants for community youth programs • City council supports a 15-year lease on space for a new youth center • Expand nonprofit training in organic food production and nutrition education • Expand Parent Home Visit Project and Parent University – strategies increasing student achievement and graduation • Partner with workforce development agency to increase pre-employment training and educate businesses about youth hiring • Partnered with a regional nonprofit to develop an urban farm stand • Peer mediation and anger management classes at four schools led to decreased suspensions and disruptions and increased test scores
Create new or improved public policies	• Student organizing reshapes discipline policy, student–teacher relationships, and maintenance procedures at the local high school • Advocate for a city parcel tax for youth with youth-generated research • Collaborated on a social host ordinance

institutional capacity to hold, nurture, and sustain this challenging work. The task is not simply giving youth voice; it is making sure that voice will be heard by focusing the goals and then building the necessary bridges to local organizations and policy makers.

Strategic focus: getting the questions right

Coalitions struggled to focus their efforts, especially in the early stages. Not only was there a tendency to hold onto too many community change priorities, but also coalition leaders conceived of *youth engagement* and *community change* as separate tasks. The coalitions with the most focused objectives built on preexisting collaboration but often struggled to integrate youth voice and priorities. Other coalitions spent most of their time and energy providing youth enrichment experiences without linking those to any overarching community change strategy.

The most promising work from the cases suggests three strategic questions whose answers will contribute clarity about how to integrate youth engagement and community change:

- Which youth are the focus of the community change effort, both as beneficiaries and as engaged participants?
- Which community transformations are high priorities, and how can they be enacted?
- What specific contributions will youth engagement provide?

The three choices are interrelated: choices about "which youth" inform prioritization of objectives and strategy, which then inform choices about whether or how to feature youth civic engagement as part of the change strategy.

Which youth?

The youth population in a community embodies a wide diversity of backgrounds and experiences – differences associated not only with ethnicity, culture, language, socioeconomic status, and interests, but also factors such as immigration status, sexual orientation, involvement with the child welfare and/or juvenile justice system, family stability, or special needs. Efforts to pursue community change on behalf of and with youth must recognize *whose* insights and concerns are represented, understanding that different youth populations may have very different experiences in the same community. The foundation initiative defined itself in terms of the needs of "all youth," but this orientation did not often translate into engagement with the most vulnerable youth (Erbstein, 2010). Grantees that did engage such youth over time demonstrated the high level of intentionality and commitment required to create safe, supportive, and meaningful settings that promoted their ongoing participation and leadership.

Which community transformations are a high priority, and how can they be enacted?

While a coalition can benefit from advertising a broad and inclusive goal – such as youth development – they must also articulate priorities that can mobilize activity to achieve specific policy or systems change objectives (Gardner, 2005; Stone et al., 2006). Choices abound. If the objective is policy change, coalitions must decide whether to strengthen the existing safety net or change the odds that youth will need it; expand the resource pie or redirect how current resources are deployed; and shape public perceptions of youth or influence youth-related legislation, rules and regulations. If the objective is systems change, they must discuss whether to build an "insider" network of service providers committed to systems change; facilitate an "outsider" community organizing strategy that builds and taps the knowledge and power of youth and their families to advocate for change; or opt for some combination of insider organizing with street connections (Burciaga & Erbstein, 2009; Noguera, Cammarota, & Ginwright, 2006; Yosso, 2005). If the objective is moving a particular community-scale indicator of youth well-being, coalitions need to consider how to institutionalize youth reflection on data. Whatever choices are made, getting the scale right is important. Coalitions can fail either by taking on too much superficial activity that does not appear to be going anywhere or by defining the problem in such broad terms that it is hard to generate a sense of momentum or progress (Weick, 1984).

Why and how to engage youth in the community change effort?

Once collaborating youth and adults have established priority community transformations and chosen strategies to effect those changes, strategic youth roles can be clarified. The findings highlight both costs and benefits of engaging youth. Among the costs are resource intensiveness; a slower pace (it takes time to build relationships, knowledge, and trust with youth); and the potential of reduced credibility in the views of some decision makers who may see youth as bringing little of real value. Corresponding benefits include:

- young people's unique insights about their own challenges and resources;
- youth energy and creativity;
- youth networks that can be mobilized to support the change effort;
- the creation of valuable leadership and social capital development opportunities for the youth themselves (building their capacity as civic actors); and
- potential for increased credibility in the eyes of decision makers who share these values.

With adequate support, young people have the capacity to take on many types of leadership roles. Across the seven community initiatives, these included speaking publicly on behalf of the coalition, helping plan and facilitate meetings, leading workshops for other youth, and other tasks. To make sure these opportunities are both beneficial to them and efficacious for the community, it is best if youth roles are purposefully aligned with community change objectives.

Creating structures that integrate youth and adults in joint decision making

Efforts to build shared leadership among youth and adults reflected trajectories set by preexisting organizational arrangements. Paradoxically, both the presence and absence of preexisting collaborative infrastructure related to youth-focused community change proved challenging, each in its own way. Where communities had little preexisting infrastructure, the initiative supported the launch of a change process that intentionally built youth voice. However, the energy, focus, and time it took to establish a working coalition made it harder to achieve short-term goals. Where previous infrastructure could be built upon, there was a greater capacity to achieve short-term goals, but more tension about how to integrate youth voice into collaboratives which had not previously included youth leaders.

The struggles also reflected the nature of the lead organization. Grantees led by service delivery organizations had to adjust their traditional orientation towards youth as service recipients to engage them as co-creators of goals and plans. By contrast, community organizing groups readily embraced the ideal of youth voice but had a steep learning curve in creating developmentally appropriate settings for youth activity.

All seven grantees eventually created a separate youth group, finding it difficult to sustain youth participation without a regular venue for informal interaction with friends and engagement in youth-oriented activities. Youth groups forged a collective youth identity, created a setting for engaging youth in decisions, and promoted ongoing interaction with adults. Although all the groups had features that were similar to traditional after-school programs, a danger of functioning solely in this fashion was that it diverted staff energy from the broader community change goals and isolated youth from adult strategy discussions.

More intentional work is needed to support the creation of venues where youth and adults participate in joint decision making. Moving beyond token or trivial youth leadership roles requires a broader strategic perspective. Consistent with the findings of previous research (Christens & Dolans, 2011; Gambone et al., 2006), the most promising strategies in these communities used principles derived from the field of community organizing (often translated as "youth organizing" when young people are the key participants). In this approach, youth work with adult allies to elicit youth perspectives on problems or opportunities, then gather data to support change alternatives, and finally make their case to decision makers. Working in this fashion, effective adult supporters of youth had the ability to nurture an ongoing cycle of action and reflection that gradually built youth skills, knowledge, and confidence. Rather than simply holding meetings to hear youth input, skilled adult allies engaged young people in thinking critically about what they were doing, why, and what could be learned from the results. Intentional conversation with youth before, during, and after activities both fostered growth among young people and furthered strategy development with respect to defined community change objectives.

Mobilizing leaders with broad-based skills and networks

Coalitions had to activate or develop adult and youth leaders with requisite skills, community legitimacy and relationships, and sustained engagement. Many youth became powerful coalition leaders who were able to recruit new participants, develop and share skills, take on increased responsibility, and become known to local leaders. Two grantees found ways to develop youth leadership assets by hiring local youth and young adults as organizers/coordinators, pairing them with more experienced leaders, and creating ladders of responsibility for professional development.

Differences in the character, background, style, and approach of adult leaders explained the level and quality of youth engagement. The effects of program staff turnover offered key evidence of this point: the same institutional setting or program structure that worked well for engaging youth under one adult leader often worked less well when a new leader took over (or vice versa). The complex work required skills rarely found in any single individual, as suggested by this list of supports requested of technical assistance providers: training in basic youth development principles; knowledge of strategies that support youth engagement/youth voice;

meeting facilitation skills (especially meetings with youth *and* adults); ability to engage with parents/caretakers across language and cultural differences; community organizing abilities with targeted youth populations and/or neighborhoods; concepts in systems/policy change and asset-based community development; ability to plan for organizational/fiscal sustainability; skill in evaluation and data gathering for results-based accountability; and knowledge of approaches used effectively in other communities.

Assembling a team with these complementary skill sets was more likely when leaders not only were experienced community developers or organizers themselves, but had also spent considerable time on the ground getting to know youth and adult social networks as well as community power brokers, politics, issues, and history. Grantees that cultivated existing local talent, instead of hiring individuals from outside the community, experienced less turnover and had an easier time establishing and maintaining strategic focus.

Summary and considerations for future research

This article has focused on how to pair high quality youth engagement with broad and effective community, policy, or systems change strategies. The comparative analysis of seven community youth development coalitions suggests that this work is quite taxing in terms of time, resources, and commitment, but worth pursuing due to the potential benefits for youth, adults, and their communities. These include observable increases in the skills, confidence and leadership of individual youth; increased integration of vulnerable youth and families and their unique insights into schools and the broader community; increased capacity of adults to foster settings that allowed youth voice to mature; increased adult appreciation of the value of young people's ideas and contributions; and small but tangible steps toward community change.

The difficulty in achieving broader community change goals in these seven cases can be attributed in part to the short 3-year time frame. But even with more time and money, many challenges would remain. As previous studies have found (Zeldin et al., 2008), this difficult work stretched boundaries and standard expectations for community leaders, organizations, funders, and young people. For leaders, it required a mix of attributes and capacities that is difficult to find: community rootedness, relationships, knowledge, and legitimacy; skills that span both youth development and community development; and access to support in extending and supplementing those skills via partnerships or technical assistance. For lead organizations where service delivery had been the main focus, it required incorporating cultural changes and staff skill development to support a new commitment to youth voice. For foundations, it required tempering the desire for quick results with patience, since the work takes more time and resources than most expect, particularly when commitments include ensuring representation of vulnerable youth populations or taking on entrenched conditions, perspectives, and interests. For youth, it required the emotional risk of building relationships with adults, operating in unfamiliar and often adult-oriented cultural and linguistic contexts, trying out new skills and making mistakes, and honestly sharing experiences of growing up in the local community. Some young people confronted even higher stakes challenges, such as negotiating differences between the coalition emphasis on youth voice and home settings where deference to adults was expected, navigating unsafe community territory to be present at meetings, and/or deciding whether to reveal immigration status.

As Christens and Dolen (2011) argued, research in this field has been bifurcated between a youth development focus on individual developmental outcomes and a community organizing focus on community-scale outcomes. Future practice and research will benefit by bringing these concerns together, integrating effective youth civic engagement methods with the broader strategic considerations reflected in the three implementation principles of strategy, structure, and leadership.

Key research questions suggested by this analysis include: What is the comparative effectiveness – with respect to both youth development and community change objectives – of relational, activity-based, and agenda-driven approaches to engaging youth in community change? Do the answers vary according to local context variables, and/or the specific youth population to be engaged? What are the characteristics of the most effective models for integrating youth and adult voices into community decision making? How might community coalitions or institutions make better use of community organizing strategies and techniques as a vehicle for integrating youth voice into institutional decisions? How do the three principles delineated here hold up in other contexts where localities seek to engage youth in community change?

By bringing community development ideas to bear in a realm often dominated by specialists in youth development, this research has identified important implementation principles that can shape more effective community practice. When combined with insights from the field of youth development, these ideas can form the foundation for more robust, place-sensitive conceptual models of youth engagement in community-scale change.

Acknowledgments

This research was funded by the Sierra Health Foundation; Director of Program Investments Diane Littlefield and Program Officer Matt Cervantes created a context where honest reflection and learning were valued. We are grateful for the cooperation of REACH leaders and participants and technical assistance staff. Graduate students James Fabionar, Whitney Wilcox, and Lisceth Cruz Carrasco and See Change Evaluation staff Melanie Moore Kubo, Ashley McKenna, and Melissa Saphir supported data collection and analysis; Cathy Lemp made major early contributions. At UC Davis, John Jones (Center for Community School Partnerships) and Carrie Matthews provided administrative support. We received helpful advice from an evaluation advisory committee: Marc Braverman (Oregon State University), Leslie Cooksy (University of Delaware), and Elizabeth Miller, Patsy Eubanks Owens, and Dina Okamoto (UC Davis). For more information on the REACH program and copies of evaluation reports, visit Sierra Health Foundation's website: www.sierrahealth.org.

Notes

1. For more information, see http://www.sierrahealth.org/doc.aspx?22.
2. The videos can be viewed at http://www.reachyouthprogram.org/youth_media. For a more complete description and analysis of the youth media work, see Wilcox and Campbell (2010).

References

Balsano, A.B. (2005). Youth civic engagement in the United States: Understanding and addressing the impact of social impediments on positive youth and community development. *Applied Developmental Science*, 9(4), 188–201.

Benson, P. (1997). *All kids are our kids: What communities must do to raise responsible and caring children and adolescents.* San Francisco, CA: Jossey-Bass.

Boyte, H.C. (2004). *Everyday politics: Reconnecting citizens and public life.* Philadelphia, PA: University of Pennsylvania Press.

Brennan, M.A., & Barnett, R.V. (Eds.). (2009). Bridging community and youth development: Exploring theory, research, and application. *Community Development, 40* [Special Issue].

Burciaga, R., & Erbstein, N. (2009). *Challenging assumptions, revealing community cultural wealth: Young adult wisdom on hope in hardship* (Healthy Youth Healthy Regions Working Paper Series). Davis, CA: Center for Regional Change, UC Davis.

Camino, L., & Zeldin, S. (2002). From periphery to center: Pathways for youth civic engagement in the day-to-day life of communities. *Applied Developmental Science, 6*(4), 213–220.

Campbell, D., Erbstein, N., Fabionar, J., Wilcox, W., & Cruz Carrasco, L. (2010, November). *Engaging youth in community change: Outcomes and lessons learned from Sierra Health Foundation's REACH Youth Program.* Davis, CA: California Communities Program, University of California, Davis.

Carlson, C. (2006). The Hampton experience as a new model for youth civic engagement. *Journal of Community Practice, 14*(1), 89–106.

Checkoway, B.N., & Gutierrez, L.M. (2006). Youth participation and community change. *Journal of Community Practice, 14*(1), 1–9.

Christens, B.D., & Dolan, T. (2011). Interweaving youth development, community development, and social change through youth organizing. *Youth & Society, 43*(2), 528–548.

Cruz Carrasco, L., & Campbell, D. (2010). *Engaging parents in a community youth development initiative* (REACH Issue Brief No. 4). Sacramento, CA: Sierra Health Foundation.

Erbstein, N. (2010). *Toward making good on "all youth": Engaging under-represented youth populations in community youth development* (REACH Issue Brief No. 6). Sacramento, CA: Sierra Health Foundation.

Evans, S., & Prilleltensky, I. (2005). Youth civic engagement: Promise and peril. In M. Ungar (Ed.), *Handbook for working with children and youth: Pathways to resilience across cultures and contexts* (pp. 405–416). Thousand Oaks, CA: Sage Publications.

Fabionar, J., & Campbell, D. (2010). *Community–school partnerships to support youth development* (REACH Issue Brief No. 2). Sacramento, CA: Sierra Health Foundation.

Ferman, B. (2005). Youth civic engagement in practice. *The Good Society, 14*, 45–50.

Flanagan, C., & Levine, P. (2010). Civic engagement and the transition to adulthood. *Future of Children, 20*(1), 159–179.

Flora, J.L., Sharp, J., Flora, C., & Newlon, B. (1997). Entrepreneurial social infrastructure and locally initiated economic development in the nonmetropolitan United States. *Sociological Quarterly, 38*, 623–645.

Gambone, M.A., Klein, A.M., & Connell, J.P. (2002). *Finding out what matters for youth: Testing key links in a community action framework for youth development.* Philadelphia, PA: Youth Development Strategies, Inc., and Institute for Research and Reform in Education.

Gambone, M.A., Yu, H.C., Lewis-Charp, H., Sipe, C.L., & Lacoe, J. (2006). Youth organizing, identity-support, and youth development agencies as avenues for involvement. *Journal of Community Practice, 14*(1), 235–253.

Gardner, S.L. (2005). *Cities, counties, kids and families: The essential role of local government.* Lanham, MD: University Press of America.

Ginwright, S., & James, T. (2002). From assets to agents of change: Social justice, organizing and youth development. *New Directions for Youth Development, 96*, 27–46.

Ginwright, S., Noguera, P., & Cammarota, J. (Eds.). 2006. *Beyond resistance! Youth activism and community change.* New York: Taylor and Francis Group.

Glaser, B.G., & Strauss, F. (1967). *The discovery of grounded theory.* Chicago, IL: Aldine Transaction.

Gray, A., & Hayes, C.D. (2008). *Understanding the state of knowledge of youth engagement financing and sustainability.* Washington, DC: The Finance Project.

Hildreth, R.W. (2000). Theorizing citizenship and evaluating public achievement. *Political Science and Politics, 33*(3), 627–632.

HoSang, D. (2006a). Beyond policy: Race, ideology and the re-imagining of youth. In S. Ginwright, P. Noguera, & J. Cammarota (Eds.), *Beyond resistance! Youth activism and community change.* New York: Routledge.

HoSang, D.W. (2006b). Family and community as the cornerstone of civic engagement: Immigrant and youth organizing in the southwest. *National Civic Review*, *95*(4), 58–61.

Hughes, D.M., & Curnan, S.P. (2000). Community youth development: A framework for action. *Community Youth Development Journal*, *1*(1), 7–11.

Irby, M., Ferber, T., Pittman, K., with Tolman, J., & Yohalem, N. (2001). *Youth action: Youth contributing to communities, communities supporting youth*. Takoma Park, MD: The Forum for Youth Investment, International Youth Foundation.

Kubisch, A.C. (2005). Comprehensive community building initiatives – Ten years later: What we have learned about the principles guiding the work. *New Directions for Youth Development*, *2005*(106), 17–26.

Lerner, R.M., & Benson, P.L. (2003). *Developmental assets and asset-building communities: Implications for research, policy and practice*. New York, NY: Kluwer Academic/Plenum Publishers.

Libby, M., Sedonaen, M., & Bliss, S. (2006). The mystery of youth leadership development: The path to just communities. *New Directions for Youth Development*, *2006*(109), 13–25.

Lincoln, Y., & Guba, E.G. (1985). *Naturalist inquiry*. Newbury Park, CA: Sage Publications.

London, J.K., Zimmerman, K., & Erbstein, N. (2003). Youth-led research and evaluation: Tools for youth, organizational, and community development. *New Directions for Evaluation*, *2003*(98), 33–45.

Nagda, B.R.A., McCoy, M.L., & Barrett, M.H. (2006). Mix it up: Crossing social boundaries as a pathway to youth civic engagement. *National Civic Review*, *95*(1), 47–56.

Noguera, P.A., Cammarota, J., & Ginwright, S. (Eds.). (2006). *Beyond resistance! Youth activism and community change*. New York: Routledge.

Perri, M. (2007). Vaughan youth cabinet: Youth participation in community planning and design. *Children, Youth, and Environments*, *17*(2), 581–593.

Pittman, K.J. (2000). Balancing the equation: Communities supporting youth, youth supporting communities. *Community Youth Development Journal*, *1*, 33–36.

Sanchez-Jankowski, M. (2002). Minority youth and civic engagement: The impact of group relations. *Applied Developmental Science*, *6*(4), 237–245.

Sherrod, L. (2003). Promoting the development of citizenship in diverse youth. *Political Science and Politics*, *36*(2), 287–292.

Sherrod, L., Flanagan, C., & Youniss, J. (2002). Dimensions of citizenship and opportunities for youth development: The what, why, when, where, and who of citizenship development. *Applied Developmental Science*, *6*(4), 264–272.

Sirianni, C. (2005, April). *Youth civic engagement: Systems change and culture change in Hampton, Virginia* (Working Paper 31). Medford, MA: The Center for Information & Research on Civic Learning and Engagement.

Stone, C., Orr, M., & Worgs, D. (2006). The flight of the bumblebee: Why reform is difficult but not impossible. *Perspectives on Politics*, *4*, 529–546.

Varney, D. (2007). Splitting the ranks: Youth as leaders. *Children, Youth, and Environments*, *17*(2), 646–673.

Watts, R.J., & Flanagan, C. (2007). Pushing the envelope on youth civic engagement: A developmental and liberation psychology perspective. *Journal of Community Psychology*, *35*(6), 779–792.

Weick, K.E. (1984). Small wins: Redefining the scale of social problems. *American Psychologist*, *39*(1), 40–49.

Weick, K.E. (1995). *Sensemaking in organizations*. Thousand Oaks, CA: Sage Publications.

Wheeler, W., & Edlebeck, C. (2006). Leading, learning, and unleashing potential: Youth leadership and civic engagement. *New Directions for Youth Development*, *2006*(109), 89–97.

Wilcox, W., & Campbell, D. 2010. *Youth-produced media in community change efforts* (REACH Issue Brief No. 3). Sacramento, CA: Sierra Health Foundation.

Yosso, T.J. (2005). Whose culture has capital? A critical race theory discussion of community cultural wealth. *Race Ethnicity and Education*, *8*(1), 69–91.

Zeldin, S., Petrokubi, J., & Camino, L. (2008, October). *Youth–adult partnerships in public action: Principles, organizational culture and outcomes*. Washington, DC: The Forum for Youth Investment.

Engaging the underserved in community leadership development: Step Up to Leadership graduates in northwest Missouri tell their stories

Wilson Majee[a], Scott Long[b] and Deena Smith[b]

[a]Community Development Program, University of Missouri Extension, Princeton, MO, USA; [b]Green Hills Community Action Agency, MO, USA

In the face of growing challenges in rural America, policy-makers, academics, and practitioners are increasingly advocating for a more homegrown approach to rural development that seeks to identify and build upon internal community assets, such as the development of community leadership and entrepreneurship capacity. An interpretive case study analysis explored the impact of a community leadership program on participants' leadership skills, their well-being, and that of their communities. Data were obtained from participant surveys and interviews with graduates of the program and professionals knowledgeable of the leadership program. Through participation in the program, participants improved their ability to interact with others; gained increased understanding of civic responsibility and awareness of local resources; improved their knowledge of community issues; and grew in self-confidence, employability, and optimism. Interaction with professionals and other community members during and outside the program created networking opportunities – bridging social capital.

Introduction

In America, a large number of rural communities are facing many challenges: jobs are declining and incomes are eroding, and their backbone – volunteers, youth, businesses, and government services – has become fragile (Miller, Gibbens, Lennon, & Wakefield, 2008). There is an enormous variety of differences between rural and urban communities – the lavish, chrome-plated hospitals, clinics, banks, and post-offices in big cities versus the spartan, bare-bones facilities in rural communities (Reid, 2009). Associated with this, is a general trend of "brain drain" from rural communities to metropolitan areas and a seemingly inevitable outflow of economic and social infrastructure. This leaves policymakers, academics and development practitioners pondering the question: How can rural communities be consolidated and even developed under these circumstances? One potential venue to influence development is "effective rural leadership that is practical and capable of addressing multifaceted issues" (Avant & Copeland, n.d.). Communities must invest in the development of their people to create a high quality of life locally and to competitively progress in today's turbulent global village (Reed-Adams, n.d.). This article is special in that it explores a leadership program that uniquely targets low-income participants. Research-based evidence on the influence of educational community leadership development programs on the capacities of people to participate in the development of their communities is spotty.

The phenomenon of leadership has been extensively explored and its characteristics and virtues well documented in the literature on leadership building (Bolton, 1991; Howell, Weir, & Cook, 1979; Kouzes & Posner, 1995; Langone & Rohs, 1995; Mills, 2005; Northouse, 1997; Pigg, 1999; Price & Behrens, 2003; Wituk, Ealey, Clark, Heiny, & Meissen, n.d.). Leadership development programs have existed for several years. Universities, community organizations, corporations, local government entities, and foundations are, independently or in partnership, devoting tremendous resources to help improve the vitality and wealth of individuals and communities through the development of local leadership capacities.

This study uses data collected through in-depth interviews, surveys, and document analysis to examine the impact of Step Up to Leadership (SUL), a community leadership program offered in the state of Missouri. Focus on SUL is premised on the assumption that it is one leadership program that has been well received, has had graduates since 2006 and that its ultimate impact would be reflected primarily in the ongoing leadership activities of its graduates. Those who want to know the impact SUL has had on participants and their communities can find that in these pages. Assessing of rural community leadership development programs is timely because, "the quest for effective leadership in rural areas is arguably the greatest challenge facing rural communities" (Avant & Copeland, n.d.). Interest in evaluating SUL stems from one major factor: a shared organizational (GHCAA, University of Missouri Extension, and Missouri Association of Community Agencies) need to assess the impact of the program in order to streamline services to better meet community needs. Findings from this study will be useful in decision-making discussions that influence the allocation of resources for community development practice, to program developers in revising the curricula to better meet the needs of community members, and to other leadership development program providers interested in offering a similar program.

Understanding community leadership

Definitions and meanings of community leadership are numerous. It has been defined as, "that which involves influence, power, and input into public decision-making over one or more spheres of activity. The spheres of activity may include an organization, an area of interest, an institution, a town, county or a region." (The National Extension Task Force, 1986) Others, Abowitz, Jayanandhan, and Woiteshek (2009) view community leadership as comprising, "the actions of citizens who convene, deliberate, inquire, collaborate, and act with the intent to improve life for fellow citizens in their communities and the larger society." (p. 1) Avolio (1999) defined it as the quality of the behavior of individuals whereby they guide people or their activities in an organized effort. However defined, the collective understanding is that community leadership "emphasizes a collaborative, ongoing, influential process based on the relationships between people" (Avant & Copeland, n.d.). It recognizes the need for community members to acquire and apply skills, through involvement in policy and decision-making processes that shape their lives (Langone & Rohs, 1995; Robinson, 1994). As a process, community leadership is interactive and fosters significant relationships between and among community members.

Several leadership models, the trait theory (Ghiselli, 1963; Stogdill, 1948), the behavioral theory (Likert, 1967; Yukl, 1998), the situational theory (Hersey & Blanchard, 1982; McGregor, 1960), and the transformational theory (Bass, 1990; Bass & Avolio, 1994) have been used to expound leadership and its development. Various key characteristics of leadership and its development in different settings (urban versus rural, organizational versus community) are highlighted in each of these models. Of particular interest to this study, is the transformational model. The approach encourages input in decision making and stresses the importance of teamwork and social relationships. Connectivity between and/or among individuals is central to the theory. It recognizes the importance of individual, group, and community networks (Chemers & Ayman, 1993; Pigg, 1999). It calls for individual input while working for the overall benefit of the community. It fosters an environment in which community members feel included and appreciated which, in turn, motivates them to enhance their own satisfaction while working to promote the good of the community (Avant & Copeland, n.d.). Transformational leadership is empowering and participatory because it promotes decision-making through local involvement and leadership. Teamwork is emphasized and the community is viewed as a system of people working together with common dreams. This leadership style creates a culture based on openness, trust, and respect, and inspires team spirit (Chemers & Ayman, 1993) and has been key in the development of community leadership programs (CLPs).

CLPs are programs aimed at creating and sustaining local leadership in order to encourage and maintain sustainable community development. Class curriculum differs from place to place but generally include the following: (a) community history, resources, and challenges; (b) focused community tours (e.g. healthcare, major businesses, and education); and (c) networking opportunities (J.W. Fanning Institute for Leadership, 2003). Program length varies from about six to nine months with an average of 72 cumulative hours of meeting time. Participants are usually professionals such as business managers, educators, and local government officials (Brungradt & Seibel, 1995; Howell et al., 1979; Langone & Rohs, 1995; Wituk, et al., n.d.).

Because CLPs have a transformational emphasis, that is they emphasize leadership as relationships rather than positions and responsibilities, they are more likely to help overcome many community residents' reluctance to "get involved" or "be a leader" (Pigg, 1999). In many communities, particularly rural areas, the reluctance of members of society to get involved in their community is a major concern that dampens any community development efforts. Providing leadership development programs that foster relationship building might alleviate the fear and unwillingness certain people have in assuming leadership roles (Avant & Copeland, n.d.). In any case, if communities are to create a high quality of life locally, and compete successfully in the new global, social, political, and economic realities, they must invest in the development of their people (Reed-Adams, n.d.). In the wake of the growing community development challenges rural America faces, the provision of community leadership development programs offers the greatest potential for sustainable development in these areas.

In a nutshell, it has been argued that CLPs offer many benefits including but not limited to, increased citizen involvement/volunteer activity (Fariborz & Ma'rof, 2008; Kincaid & Knop, 1992), increased networking among participants and/or community groups (Langone & Rohs, 1992) and increased confidence and leadership skills (Rohs & Langone, 1993; Whent & Leising, 1992). However, in today's ever-changing societies, the ability of CLPs to promote leadership skills remains under scrutiny. Thus, continued local research to evaluate the effectiveness of CLPs in building local leadership capacities is needed, especially in rural communities.

Methods

Case study

The research discussed herein sets out to further explore the influence of CLPs on participants and their communities. It is based on a case study of a community leadership program, called SUL, offered throughout the state of Missouri through Community Action Agencies and in partnership with the University of Missouri Extension. SUL began in 2006 and had, at the time of research, a total of 499 graduates of which 401(80%) were women. Of the 499 graduates, 102 (84 women and 18 men) were in the Green Hills Community Action Agency (GHCAA) region, one of the 10 community action agencies offering SUL in the state. GHCAA, working in partnership with the state, counties, communities, and other agencies provides a range of human and economic development services and activities aimed at assisting low-income people in their efforts to become self-reliant by empowering them to achieve the knowledge, skills, and motivations needed to build strong families and communities. Located in north central Missouri, GHCAA serves the predominantly rural counties of Caldwell, Daviess, Grundy, Harrison, Linn, Livingston, Mercer, Putnam, and Sullivan, with limited services in Carroll, Chariton, Clinton, DeKalb, and Ray Counties (GHCAA, n.d.). Each of the counties has population less than 20,000 people.

SUL is a 12-week course designed to nurture leadership skills and encourage participants to make a difference in their communities through civic involvement. The program has 12 sessions presented, once a week, in the following order: (1) come as you are, (2) planning for your passion, (3) team up, (4) understanding diversity, (5) embracing diversity, (6) all aboard – the legalities, (7) all aboard – the practicalities, (8) meeting manners and meeting matters, (9) conflict as opportunity, (10) speak up, speak out, (11) funding the way, and (12) stepping out. Each of the session lasts 3 h with about 12–18 participants on average. Each session has activities and assignments that participants perform during and after session (Reed-Adams, Donahue & Duncan, 2005).

The curriculum, a Cadillac of training programs, intertwines two learning goals – to provide (a) "content learning about specific topics a novice board member might need to know" and (b) "a learning environment where participants can develop self-awareness and enhance their understanding about human nature and relationships" (Reed-Adams et al., 2005). For example, the first session, come as you are, is designed to help participants explore interests, strengths, and challenges; identify competencies and skills that lead to empowerment; identify basic human needs; and recognize why grassroots participation on boards, committees and in the community is important. Session 11, funding the way, teaches graduates how to identify and apply for funding. The session includes an opportunity for course graduates to competitively apply for mini-grants ($250.00 each) through GHCAA to start or contribute to efforts that address conditions of poverty in their communities. The last session, stepping out, provides an opportunity for participants to reflect on knowledge gained, enhance partnership networks, demonstrate public speaking ability, and sustain the inspiration (Reed-Adams et al., 2005).

The program supports participants by helping with necessities such as food, child care, and transportation. Cost for dinner is estimated at $5.00 per person per session. A stipend of $20.00 per person per session to cover babysitting and/or mileage reimbursement at 38cents per mile is offered to income qualifying participants. However, participants are encouraged to buy the program manual at $100.00 a piece. Instructors vary from county to county, and some volunteer while others are paid for both their time and mileage expenses.

What makes SUL unique is that it targets low-income participants. It tries to bridge the gap in leadership development between the "haves" and "have-nots" by giving a voice to low-income people. For a long time this sector of the economy has been left behind in local leadership and decision-making processes. For many low-income participants, the course is their first opportunity to learn about characteristics of great leaders, public speaking, dealing with conflict, the art of listening, and how to work well with others (Step Up to Leadership, n.d.). It is intended to help people identify how they want to contribute to their communities and teaches them techniques to turn their strengths and passions into action.

Data collection

To obtain impact data, three types of data collection were employed: semi-structured interview schedules, a written survey, and document analysis. To initiate contact with SUL graduates, a letter of intent to assess the impact of SUL program was mailed to potential research participants. The letter also served as an invitation to participate in the research. All interested SUL program graduates were encouraged to sign the consent forms so that arrangements could be made for interviews.

A semi-structured interview schedule developed by the researchers, in consultation with experts actively involved in the program, was used. Experts included University Extension Specialists; community and business leaders; and instructors/facilitators of the SUL program. However, as an emergent interview schedule, questions were revised, added and dropped depending on participants' ability to answer the questions and the relevance of the question given the participants' experiences.

Interviewees were selected through purposive and snowballing approaches. That is to say, as much as possible, interviews were conducted with all the people whose names were frequently mentioned during interviews with the purposively selected SUL graduates. The specific theoretical population that we were interested in studying was the 102 graduates of SUL program in the nine county region served by GHCAA. A sample of 40 people were interviewed, 30 graduates of the program and 10 professionals. Professionals consisted of University of Missouri Extension specialists, and faith-based organization, business and community leaders knowledgeable about the program, and all were from the GHCAA region. Some taught sections of the program, others provided services to the low-income participants. As with SUL graduates, professionals were selected purposively depending on their knowledge of and involvement in the program. On average, interviews with program graduates, lasted 1 h, and were audio taped. All interviews were conducted by the principal investigator. The triangulation of research participants was intentionally designed to enhance both the credibility and completeness of our findings. Bringing together the experiences of all these people provided a holistic understanding of the impact of the program.

Survey questions were constructed by the Missouri Association of Community Action Agencies in partnership with University of Missouri Extension Specialists. Information requested included demographic information (age, gender, education, household income, and assets); a comparison of before and after SUL in regards to leadership roles, reliability, openness, honesty; and participation in business and social activities. The 30 graduates who participated in the interviews also completed a survey. All 30 questionnaires mailed out were completed and returned. The response rate was high because surveys were either completed during interviews or participants were, during other community activities, constantly reminded to complete and return the survey.

Document review was used to supplement survey and interview data. Prior to the interviewing process, publications such as newspapers, end of session and program evaluations, attendance registers, volunteer hours, and SUL curriculum were analyzed. These documents provided information related to the research questions. For example, end of program evaluations were used to measure attitudes of participants about the program, while volunteer hours gave clues of the community activities in which graduates were involved. Other data collected from documents included history of the program in the region and state, participant turnover, and documented benefits enjoyed by participants.

Analyses

As with qualitative research involving in-depth interviewing, data analysis took place throughout the study. Preliminary analysis occurred primarily after on-site data collection ended and during the transcription of interviews. Building the road as we traveled enabled us to focus and shape the study as it proceeded, thereby seeking deeper understanding of emerging themes. Building on the preliminary data, final analysis entailed putting "into one category all the material from all the interviews that speaks to one concept or theme" (Rubin & Rubin, 1995, p. 226). Data analyses were conducted by all three investigators in order to improve inter-coder reliability. We individually, and later as a team, compared material within categories to discover "variations in" and "connections between" themes (Rubin & Rubin, 1995, p. 227) and between the different experiences of participants.

Coding of the interview transcripts began by labeling concepts within field notes, interview transcripts, and document review notes. Initially we coded for expressions (concepts) that stood out in the text material. For example, we associated the following codes with leadership development: (a) self-knowledge, (b) confidence, (c) self-worth, (d) community involvement, (e) networking, (f) speaking up (voice), (g) empowerment, and (h) teamwork. Later, in focused coding, material was compared across categories to discern patterns and consistency. The goal of final analysis was to "integrate the themes and concepts into one meaning" (Rubin & Rubin, 1995, p. 227) that would offer an accurate, detailed, yet subtle interpretation of the data.

Quantitative data collected through the survey were used to support or contradict data collected from interviews and documents. We used descriptive analyses such as percentages and proportions to generate insights.

Findings

The primary purpose of this article is to examine the impact the community leadership program, SUL, has had in the lives of those who attended and graduated from the program and the impact that in turn, has had on the community. We present our findings by first describing the stories of four interviewees in detail and then discussing the rest of our observations from a broader perspective. Measures were taken to ensure that possible identifying factors for interviewees are minimal.

Nancy Gore

Nancy was born in 1963 into a middle-class family with two children. Growing up, life was as good as it could be. She obtained a teaching degree and began working at a college. However, a few years into her marriage, she became involved in alcohol and drug abuse. In 1993, she was arrested for manufacturing drugs and served with a 17-year suspended execution of sentence (SES). Her marital life became character-ized by frequent episodes of domestic violence and in 1996 she divorced her husband. Cast into the street, a single mother, a felon, and unemployed, Nancy moved into a women's shelter, where she stayed for eight months. Life became unbearable and in 2000 she was diagnosed with breast cancer. It was during these doldrums that Nancy was invited to participate in SUL. Recounting how she felt about the invitation, she favored an economic explanation:

> I had no money coming into the household, had bills that needed to be paid, had a child to look after and I needed groceries. So when the offer was given that there is a $25.00 money voucher that went with that [participation in the program] for a stipend, I said that's okay. It was up to $250.00 if you took the class for 12 weeks and I knew I could commit to the 12 weeks, so that was a lot of money for me at the time. So the real reason I took the class was for the money. (N. Gore, personal communication, December 12, 2009).

However, during the program Nancy soon became engaged, empowered, and very active in community activities such as holding board positions, volunteering with local community organizations on a call basis, and working at a food pantry and community garden. She does not regret having taken part in the program:

> I am a single mom, a felon, and a cancer patient. I had gotten overwhelmed with all these depressing issues ... and had lost hope. The program gave me a chance to get my voice back, to be self-confident and self-worth, ... [it] brought the community back and made me realize I had a role to play. I have been able to give a voice on a lot of different organizations. That probably wouldn't have all happened had it not been for SUL. (N. Gore, personal communication, December 12, 2009).

The food pantry she co-ordinates serves about 250 clients per month (Grundy County Food Pantry Report, n.d.). The garden has 136 community growers, of which 106 (78%) are considered low-income, that is living below the poverty line (Grundy County Community Garden Reports, n.d.). The garden is divided into two sections: one supplying the food pantry with fresh produce and the other for community to grow for their consumption.

Mike Owens

Mike, 50 years old at the time of the study, grew up on the East Coast and had resided in rural Missouri with his wife and young son for over seven years. The years prior to his participation in SUL were characterized by a checkered work history, moving from one construction job to another. Explaining the period prior to SUL training, Mike admits that he was going through a "lot of kick in the butt types of things – failures." (M. Owens, personal communication, December 14, 2009). After being turned down for several job openings, Mike began to feel resentment toward the local area and its companies and seriously doubted his own abilities since no one would hire him. It was during this period that he heard about and was invited to participate in the program. SUL changed Mike's perceptions and life, as he passionately acknowledged:

> They [SUL] educated me to see the value in myself . . . and in others. I was going through some tough times, and the program helped me not to feel sorry for myself. It opened doors for me to rub elbows with some good people with money and businesses. . . . It brought me closer to community where before I was hiding from the community. I didn't know how to act. I am now a volunteer, volunteering in the community, and World Changers and Habitat for Humanity. (M. Owens, personal communication, December 14, 2009).

Mike is definitely not "hiding" any more. He is actively involved in his church, World Changers, Celebrate Recovery, and Habitat for Humanity. He is now a board member on the local food pantry and senior citizen tax boards. He also ran for the local nursing home board as he is very passionate about helping the elderly. Since graduating from the program in 2006, Mike has had steady employment as a crew leader/member on a construction crew for a local not-for-profit housing agency. Explaining the impact of the program had on Mike, one of his supervisors said:

> Mike did have the kind of employment history that was sort of all over the place. However, he had just completed the SUL program and seemed to have a renewed sense of purpose. From what I know of the SUL program it takes a lot of commitment and perseverance for someone to finish it, so that told me that he [Mike] had the capacity to stick with something. He obviously had the construction skills . . . it was just not knowing about the "soft" skills that worried me. Him completing that program reassured me that he could work here and be successful. (G. Gault, personal communication, January 20, 2010).

Ashley Moonlight

Aged 38, at the time of the interview, Ashley described her childhood years as "rough." Born to an alcoholic and abusive father, Ashley witnessed the divorce of her parents when she was only nine years old. With her father gone, her mom continued to struggle to raise her and her two siblings. Fortunately, her grandfather helped the family and ingrained in Ashley the love of reading she has to this day. In 1990, Ashley graduated from high school and signed on with the Navy in the same year. However, she discovered that she was pregnant, a discovery that ended her plans for joining the military. With her eyes welling with tears she narrated, "Over the next several years, I worked here and there doing different jobs" (A. Moonlight, personal communication, January 19, 2010).

She had two more children over the next few years. Life got worse for her and her family on a daily basis and in 2006 she was incarcerated for two and half years because of drug abuse. When she was released from prison, she got a job as a welder and began trying to re-build her life. Struggling to educate, cloth, feed, and shelter her three children, Ashley went into her local community action agency (GHCAA) to get help. While at the GHCAA she shared her life experience. GHCAA staff encouraged her to go back to college and complete her criminal justice degree for which she was only two courses shy of finishing. Ashley buckled down and went back to school with help from the GHCAA. She was also invited to participate in SUL. Looking back to how her participation in the program changed her life she pointed out:

> Before I took the SUL training I was in poverty and didn't think my opinion mattered. I felt like I wasn't good enough to talk to certain people. I would never approach anybody [in leadership position] because my mind set was I didn't have the access. Afterwards now I talk to anybody . . . . almost on a daily basis I talk with the ex Mayor, the Chief of Police, the deputy sheriff, and/or the commissioners. It [SUL program] gave me a voice. It definitely changed my life.
> (A. Moonlight, personal communication, January 19, 2010).

With her new skills, Ashley has become very active in the community and works with others to make it a better place to live. She now works for a domestic violence shelter and uses her skills to help victims of domestic violence become survivors and establish new lives. Whilst working full time, Ashley is finishing her Bachelor of Arts degree in criminal justice administration. The other two projects she leads, a county cultural fair, and a youth drug and alcohol prevention group were each awarded a grant for $5,000 in 2010. The county cultural fair group promotes celebration of diversity, thereby, teaching tolerance for people perceived as "different" and showing their commonalities. The youth drug and alcohol prevention group works in partnership with the local school district and YMCA to organize activities such as family–fun night and awareness activities.

Katie Evans

Katie, aged 66, was born one of six children in a family that struggled with poverty. Katie described her childhood as "not nice." Her father and two step-fathers were alcoholics and abuse took place in the home. She also recalled growing up in a home where poverty always lurked in the shadows pouncing on them, forcing them to go hungry because there was often very little food in the house. At 17, she dropped out of school and got married as an escape from the dreadful life she was living. In 1984, at the age of 39, she obtained her General Education Development (GED) which she had promised herself she would do before she turned 40.

Married life was much better than her childhood years. Unfortunately, as if growing up poor was not enough of a curse, Katie's health began to deteriorate – she was diagnosed with degenerative disc disease, Type II diabetes, peripheral neuropathy, and asthma. Although her husband continued to work, his income was not enough to meet the bills. Katie and her husband were forced to seek assistance from GHCAA. She and her husband moved into an energy efficient home that had been built by the agency and that reduced their utility bills significantly. She was later invited to participate in the SUL program. Appreciating the impact the program had had in her life she said:

> Because I didn't have much growing up, it [SUL] opened my eyes to see that I had more to offer than I realized. I learned that people come from different backgrounds and I learned how to work with them all. I feel that SUL empowered me. I've always felt like I didn't matter and I learned that I do matter. Knowledge gives power. I found out things about myself that I didn't realize. It gave me a sense of more confidence. (K. Evans, personal communication, January 13, 2010).

Katie explained that because of what she learned through SUL, she is now able to act on some needs she sees in her community – people needing help with food. With a smile on her face she said, "I grew up being hungry and I never wanted to see anyone else go hungry" (K. Evans, personal communication, January 13, 2010). With the skills she learned through SUL and working with other community members, Katie participated in establishing a food supplement program in her area through the Angel Food Ministries. Through this program she provided a resource for anyone in the area to pay less for food. The Angel Food Ministries sells food such as meat, vegetables, and desserts at a third of what it costs to buy it in stores. The local chapter started in 2006 and serves over 100 families every month. She also organizes "bake sales" and "cook outs" to raise money to support some of the programs offered at GHCAA. She continues to work with GHCAA serving on the board and volunteering at community events.

Although only the stories of four interviewees are highlighted earlier, most (35 of the 40) interviewees expressed similar sentiments about the program. According to survey data summarized in Table 1, 70% of interviewees became more aware of themselves (their abilities and limitations) after going through the program, 63% improved their general confidence in themselves and their environment, 57% felt more empowered, able to work in teams, and prepared to engage in community activities. 54% of informants claimed to have gained their "voices" back. Further, data from interviews with program facilitators spoke to the same observations. According to one program facilitator, "SUL program has changed the lives of many of its participants." (O. Harrison, personal communication, December 18, 2009).

Those who were critical of the program felt that it gave them skills but did not connect them with any opportunities to apply the skills. As Givens, a 42-year-old

Table 1. Leadership skills indicators selected from survey data ($n = 30$).

Indicator	Change (%)		
	Negative	No change	Positive
Self-knowledge	0	30	70
Empowerment	3	30	57
Confidence	3	34	63
Community involvement	3	40	57
Speaking up	3	43	54
Teamwork	0	43	57

woman, pointed out, "Yes, the program gave us skills, but what do you do with the skills if there are no opportunities.... I wish something more could be done" (personal communication, December 14, 2009). The general feeling among this group of people is that the program needs to create an internship-like format where graduates will be connected to volunteer, and/or economic opportunities. They recommended a shift in the allocation of resources within the program more towards creating opportunities and linking graduates to such opportunities and less on offering the program annually. About 10% of the graduates felt that the material covered in a session was too much as one submitted, "It's hard to absorb a lot of information in a short time" (X. Givens, personal communication, December 14, 2009).

Discussion

SUL program targets low-income people. Low-income people often lack the necessary capabilities and entitlements to satisfy their needs and aspirations. They live without economic opportunities and social relationships that the rich or better-off take for granted. Poverty robs people of their voice, self-identity, self-worth, self-confidence all of which affect their ability and willingness to interact with others. They are often "exposed to ill treatment by institutions of the state and society and are powerless to influence key decisions affecting their lives" (World Bank, n.d., p. 1). The experiences of SUL participants are both surprising and instructive. This study identified several components of SUL that are critical in building community leaders in rural and poor communities.

One key component in terms of building community leadership capacity is allowing potential leaders the opportunity to see other viewpoints and value systems of persons that may be contrary to their own. Since most traditional leaders in a community are middle-class and originally from that community, it is often difficult for someone that does not fit that mold, to break through and acquire leadership positions within the community. Mike's experience fits that bill. As he says, he "married into Missouri". He did not have the over-time developed relationships to call on to find employment or get help with the broken down car or to help replace the stove that went out. An interesting benefit of SUL that Mike noted was that even though he felt that his family situation was the most "down and out," after hearing what other SUL participants had gone through, he quickly realized it could be worse. As he says, "to hear some of the stories that were said in the SUL, I wasn't going through half of what some people were going through" (M. Owens, personal communication, December 14, 2009). When people interact they share information and increase their knowledge of one another, of local human resources, and their appreciation of diverse perspectives on issues. An individual who sees things through other lenses is more likely to be open to working with others for the good of the community.

Another key component of community leadership development program that SUL promotes is the creation fertile ground on which to alleviate the "fear and unwillingness" most low-income community members have in taking up leadership roles. As one participant pointed out, "I now have the confidence to step up......patience is a virtue and it's one of the things SUL teaches you" (P. Battles, personal communication, December 14, 2009). Despondence feeds on fear, so eradicating the fear helps bring discouraged or hesitant leaders to the fore in community leadership. The experiences of Nancy, Mike, Ashley, Katie, and many of the participants in this study all support this claim. Literature on community participation suggests that engaging community members in leadership leads to community development projects that are "more responsive to the needs of the poor...more responsive government and better delivery of public goods and services, better maintained community assets, and a more informed and involved citizenry" (Mansuri & Rao, 2003). When community members emerge from their fear and have the confidence to become community leaders, they provide important information about community needs and the resolution preferences.

A third critical characteristic of the SUL program is the opportunity to help community members empower themselves to influence the decision-making processes in their community. Not only did SUL graduates express strong desires to get things done, they actually acted on them. SUL graduates engaged themselves in a variety of community service roles, ranging from employment at local libraries, coordinating community projects such as the community garden and food pantry, to serving on different organizational boards. This pool of servant leaders is helping transform the socio-economic landscape of the GHCAA service region through building teams of committed citizens to shape, not fear, the future. One example of this work was through collaboration with the Missourians to End Poverty initiative. At the time of the study, several program graduates were involved in building community empowerment collaborations where community members were learning about poverty and identify an (some) issue(s) they would work on as an effort to reduce poverty at a local level. This collaborative work demonstrates the direct impact many SUL graduates have on their community.

A fourth trait of SUL is its ability to foster the development of social capital of both a bonding and bridging nature among participants and other influential people in the community. Program graduates confirmed to have built relationships with other participants and professionals affiliated with the program. "It opened my eyes to a lot of things.... helped broaden the horizon on the fact of how to approach different people" (P. Battles, Interview, December 14, 2009) echoing Mike's experience, "It opened doors for me to rub elbows with some good people with money and businesses...." (M. Owens, personal communication, December 14, 2009). These networks have had a ripple effect of opening "wider doors" for program graduates to access community resources. Connection to resources improves community engagement and development (Majee & Hoyt, 2009, 2010).

In short, SUL demonstrates beneficial influence on both its graduates, and on their communities. Program participants have benefited from their involvement in the leadership program through increased self awareness, confidence, empowerment, community involvement, teamwork, and ability to voice their concerns. These human capital gains translate into community benefits as the graduates put their skills to practice. The program provides the greatest multiplier effect to mobilize human resources to build a sustainable future. Community gardens improve the availability of healthy food and reduce physical inactivity among community garden members. Food pantries increase food accessibility to many. Domestic violence shelters protect vulnerable populations in the community, and home construction targeted at low-income households help reduce housing expenses and homelessness. Despite these benefits some participants felt that the bridges the program builds are not strong enough to make communities stand up, stand out, and stand together in the twenty-first century.

Implications for community development

In the face of continued fractures in the backbone of rural communities (brain drain, limited volunteerism, business closures, etc.), this study demonstrates the benefits of leadership development programs that are people and place centered. For the transition from a socio-economic challenging situation to economic mainstream to happen, "effective rural leadership that is practical and capable of addressing multifaceted issues" (Avant & Copeland, n.d.) must be developed.

In rural areas where people fear leadership roles because of their low-income status, it becomes necessary to view the provision of tools for empowerment of the poor as the crucial requirement for a sustainable solution to community development: poverty and hunger reduction, fighting homelessness, domestic violence reduction, etc. Empowerment is defined here as the ability of people, in particular the least privileged, to: (a) have access to productive resources that enable them to increase their earnings and obtain the goods and services they need; and (b) participate in the development process and the decisions that affect them (World Bank, 2002). This can be achieved when local community members work together and learn that they can rely on themselves and on their ability to act collectively to improve their personal circumstances and the well-being of their community (Hoyt, unpublished CLUSA Paper).

Evidence from the SUL evaluation suggests that the program enables members to gain skills and resources that help them participate in networks beyond their families and friends. The variation in the manner with which graduates from the program pursued opportunities for engagement/involvement substantiates Bradshaw's (2006) notion that individuals who make "better choices" and "work hard" are more likely to improve their well-being than those who lack these traits. Nancy, Mike, Ashley, and Katie are all good examples of people who embraced opportunities and worked hard to change their welfare and that of the community.

However, from a research perspective, the study offers several questions for further research. The study focused on only nine (out of 115) counties in one part of the state. Of the 499 graduates in the state, only 30 (6%) were interviewed. Questions that yearn for answers include: To what extent do the stories in this study reflect the impact of the program in other rural regions of the state? Is the program equally effective with low-income participants in an urban setting? Does the community environment have effect on program process and outcomes? Does targeting low-income participants bridge the gap for community leaders in rural areas? What is the impact of participation incentives to the overall effectiveness of the program? As a case study based on a qualitative methodology, it is not the intention of this article to generalize observations to other communities where SUL is or is not offered. Rather, research investigating the impact of the program across the state would provide further important insights into the overall effectiveness of the program.

Conclusion

This study used in-depth interviews, document analysis, and survey data to explore the impact of a community leadership development program in Missouri. SUL program was designed with the goal of helping low-income people identify how they want to contribute to their communities and teaching them techniques to turn their strengths and passions into action. Findings from the study suggest that the program has had significant success in meeting these goals through changing levels of confidence, self-knowledge, speaking up, teamwork, and willingness and actual participation in community activities. This is attributed to the program's ability to foster relationship building among participants and between participants and facilitators irrespective of their backgrounds. Program graduates have become better contributing members of society.

Acknowledgements

The authors would like to acknowledge all research participants for the time and support they put into this research. Comments from all those who reviewed this manuscript are greatly appreciated. This research was funded by Green Hills Community Action Agency.

References

Abowitz, K.K., Jayanandhan, S.R., & Woiteshek, S. (2009). *Public and community-based leadership education*. A White Paper sponsored by the Wilks Leadership Institute, Miami University. Retrieved from http://community.muohio.edu/wilks/sites/edu.wilks/files/Wilks%20Public%20Leadership%20Paper,%208.4.09_2.pdf

Avant, F., & Copeland, S. (n.d.). *Leadership in rural America: Breathing new vitality into rural communities*. Retrieved from http://www.socwk.utah.edu/rural/pdf/6-B.pdf

Avolio, B. (1999). *Full leadership development: Building the vital forces in organization*. Thousand Oaks, CA: Sage Publications.

Bass, B. (1990). From transactional to transformational leadership: Learning to share the vision. *Organizational Dynamics, 18*, 19–31.

Bass, B.M., & Avolio, B.J. (Eds.). (1994). *Improving organizational effectiveness through transformational leadership*. Thousand Oaks, CA: Sage Publications.

Bolton, E.B. (1991). Developing local leaders: Results of a structured learning experience. *Journal of the Community Development Society, 21*(1), 119–143.

Bradshaw, T. (2006). Theories of poverty and antipoverty programs in community development. *Perspectives on Poverty, Policy & Place, 3*, Winter 2006. Retrieved from http://www.rprconline.org/Perspectives/Perspectivesvol3n4.pdf, Rural Policy Research Institute.

Brungardt, C.L., & Seibel, N. (1995). *Assessing the effectiveness of community leadership programs*. Kansas Leadership Forum Publication Series. Kansas Leadership Forum, Kansas, USA.

Chemers, M.M., & Ayman, R. (1993). *Leadership theory and research: Perspectives and directions*. San Diego, CA: Academic Press.

Green Hills Community Action Agency. (GHCAA, n.d.). Retrieved from http://www.ghcaa.org.

Fariborz, A., & Ma'rof, B.R. (2008). Barriers to community leadership toward tourism development in Shiraz, Iran. *European Journal of Social Sciences, 7*, 158–164.

Ghiselli, E. (1963). The validity of management traits in relation to occupational level. *Personnel Psychology, 16*, 109–113.

Grundy County Food Pantry Report. (n.d.). Unpublished report obtained from Green Hills Community Action Agency.

Hersey, P., & Blanchard, K.H. (1982). *Management of organizational behavior: Utilizing human resources*. Englewood Cliffs, NJ: Prentice-Hall.

Howell, R.E., Weir, I.L., & Cook, A.K. (1979). *Public affairs leadership development*. Pullman: Washington State University, Rural Sociology.

Hoyt, A. (n.d.). *CLUSA cooperative development paper*. Unpublished: obtained from A. Hoyt.

J.W. Fanning Institute for Leadership. (2003). *Survey of adult community leadership program content*. Atlanta, GA: University of Georgia.

Kincaid, J.M., Jr. & Knop, E.C. (1992). *Insights and implications from the Colorado rural revitalization project, 1988–1991: A final evaluation report*. Fort Collins: Center for Rural Assistance, Colorado State University.

Kouzes, J.M., & Posner, B.Z. (1995). *The leadership challenge: How to keep getting extraordinary things done in organizations* (2nd ed.). San Francisco: Jossey-Bass.

Langone, C.A., & Rohs, F.R. (1992). Community leadership, a force for future change: An impact assessment of Georgia's community leadership – a county perspective program. Athens: Cooperative Extension, University of Georgia.

Langone, C.A., & Rohs, F.R. (1995). Community leadership development: Process and practice. *Journal of the Community Development Society, 26,* 252–267.

Likert, R. (1967). *The human organization: Its management and value.* New York: McGraw-Hill.

Majee, W., & Hoyt, A. (2009). Building community trust through cooperatives: A case study of a worker-owned homecare cooperative. *Journal of Community Practice, 17,* 444–463.

Majee, W., & Hoyt, A. (2010). Are worker-owned cooperatives the brewing pots for social capital? *Journal of the Community Development Society, 41,* 417–430.

Mansuri, G., & Rao, V. (2003). *Evaluating community-based and community-driven development: A critical review of the evidence.* Retrieved from http://www.cbnrm.net/pdf/mansuri_g_001_cddfinal.pdf

McGregor, D. (1960). *The human side of enterprise.* New York: McGraw-Hill.

Miller, M., Gibbens, B., Lennon, C., & Wakefield, M. (2008). *North Dakota flex program & critical access hospital state rural health plan.* Retrieved from http://ruralhealth.und.edu/projects/flex/pdf/state_rural_health_plan112608.pdf

Mills, R.C. (2005). Sustainable community change: A new paradigm for leadership in community revitalization efforts. *National Civic Review, 94,* 9–16.

Northouse, P.G. (1997). *Leadership: Theory and practice.* Thousand Oaks, CA: Sage Publications.

Pigg, K.E. (1999). Community leadership and community theory: A practical synthesis. *Journal of the Community Development Society, 30,* 196–212.

Price, R.H., & Behrens, T. (2003). Working Pasteur's Quadrant: Harnessing science and action for community change. *American Journal of Community Psychology, 31,* 219–223.

Reed-Adams, J. (n.d.). *Step Up to Leadership.* Retrieved from http://www.communityaction.org/STEP%20Up%20to%20Leadership.aspx

Reed-Adams, J., Donahue, G., & Duncan, M. (2005). *A Facilitator's Guide to Step Up to Leadership.* Columbia, MO: University of Missouri Extension.

Reid, T.R. (2009). *The Healing of America.* New York: Penguin Press.

Robinson, J.W. (1994). Ten basic principles of leadership in community development organizations. *Journal of the Community Development Society, 25*(1), 44–48.

Rohs, F.R., & Langone, C.A. (1993). Assessing leadership and problem-solving skills and their impacts in the community. *Evaluation Review, 17*(1), 109–115.

Rubin, H.J., & Rubin, I.S. (1995). *Qualitative interviewing: The art of hearing data.* California: Sage Publications.

Step Up to Leadership Module. (n.d.). Retrieved from http://www.communityaction.org/STEP%20Up%20to%20Leadership.aspx

Stogdill, R.M. (1948). Personal factors associated with leadership: A survey of the literature. *Journal of Psychology, 25,* 35–71.

The National Extension Task Force on Community Leadership. (1986). *Community leadership development: Implications for extension.* University Park, Pennsylvania: Northeast Regional Center for Rural Development.

Whent, L.S., & Leising, J.G. (1992). A twenty-year evaluation of the California agricultural leadership program. *Journal of Agricultural Education, 33,* 32–39.

Wituk, S., Ealey, S., Clark, M.J., Heiny, P., & Meissen, G. (n.d.). *Community development through community leadership programs: Insights from a statewide community leadership initiative.* Retrieved from http://209.190.249.66/assets/library/159_2005communitydevelopmentt.pdf

World Bank (n.d.). Attacking Poverty: Opportunity, Empowerment, and Security. Retrieved from http://siteresources.worldbank.org/INTPOVERTY/Resources/WDR/overview.pdf

World Bank. (2002). *Empowerment and poverty reduction: A sourcebook for World Bank staff.* Washington, DC: World Bank.

Yukl, G.A. (1998). *Leadership in organizations.* Upper Saddle River, NJ: Prentice Hall.

Can leadership development act as a rural poverty alleviation strategy?

Ryan Allen[a] and Paul R. Lachapelle[b]

[a]Hubert H. Humphrey School of Public Affairs, University of Minnesota, USA; [b]Department of Political Science, Montana State University, USA

Though it is a pervasive problem, relatively little research focuses on rural poverty and leadership initiatives designed to alleviate rural poverty. Using a comparative case study approach, this article assesses community-level change in rural communities in Montana and Minnesota that participated in Horizons, a leadership development program that seeks to encourage community action to reduce poverty. We focus on the effects of various strategies for Horizons implementation in Montana and Minnesota as a possible explanation for different community-level outcomes experienced in these states. We argue that different methods of Horizons implementation influenced the skills and knowledge that coaches brought to their communities and also helped to determine how receptive communities were toward working with coaches. Research results also indicate that relatively minor investments in leadership development can yield dramatic changes in a community's capacity to identify and address problems.

Introduction

Research on poverty in the United States focuses predominantly on urban (Jargowsky, 1997) and suburban (Holliday & Dwyer, 2009) settings despite scholarship showing poverty is highest and most persistent in rural areas (Weber, Jensen, Miller, Mosley, & Fisher, 2005). To some extent, the research emphasis on urban and suburban areas is relevant given that rural areas have comparatively far fewer residents. On the other hand, rural areas tend to have low population densities and substantial distances between people and services compared to urban and suburban areas. For rural areas, these characteristics may exacerbate some of the other problems often found in poor communities, including long histories (including generational) of poverty, recent demographic changes, a lack of local expertise to address poverty, inadequate local governance structures, and a lack of trust between community members (Erickson, Reid, Nelson, O'Shaughnessy, & Berube, 2008). Given the particular circumstances of poverty in rural America, programs that seek to address this condition will have to be exceptionally innovative and creative.

The fundamental question guiding this research is, can a leadership development program reduce poverty in a community, and if so, how can this program be best implemented and evaluated? Funded by the Northwest Area Foundation (NWAF), the Horizons program seeks to address rural poverty by promoting local leadership and focusing community action on poverty reduction strategies. Drawing upon the power of public discourse (Barber, 1984; Dewey, 1927) and an assets-based community development approach (Kretzmann & McKnight, 1993), the Horizons program has been implemented in nearly 300 communities in seven states during an eight-year period (2003–2010). The Horizons program guides communities through conversations about poverty; helps to develop local leadership; facilitates the creation of a community vision; and implements actions and evaluates outcomes toward making the vision a reality. As such, Horizons does not focus solely on economic development or human capital accumulation strategies that are more typically associated with poverty alleviation in the US. Instead, it focuses on leadership development to provide community residents with the skills to self-design and implement poverty reduction programs.

Despite a desired uniform program design by the NWAF, the experiences of Horizons communities within and across states have varied tremendously. Some communities have embraced the spirit of Horizons that stresses communicative dialogue; the expansion of voices in the community visioning and planning process; and a focus on collective action via relational leadership. At the same time, other communities have failed to meaningfully incorporate these aspects of Horizons. In addition, some action plans produced by Horizons communities lack direct connections to reducing poverty, while other action plans include initiatives that squarely address poverty. A large part of assessing the relationship between Horizons and community-level change is determining the factors that account for the varied experiences and outcomes in Horizons communities.

This article focuses on factors that explain variation in how communities participating in Horizons approached community-level leadership and problem-solving. We focus on these issues instead of actual poverty reduction for two reasons. First, the task of tracing the causal effect of a single program on a problem as intractable as poverty is exceptionally difficult and likely made even more difficult by the presence of dynamic exogenous factors, such as changes in the economy. Second, given the short amount of time that has elapsed since the completion of Horizons in these communities it is more appropriate to focus on intermediate outcomes. Thus, this article has two primary contributions to an understanding of community-level change. First, the article offers a detailed description of a relational leadership development program outside of an organizational context, something that is relatively scarce in the leadership literature. Second, the article makes the case that a relational leadership development program can enhance the capacity of communities to acknowledge and address seemingly intractable issues, like poverty.

The remainder of this article is divided into four sections. The first section reviews the literature on relational leadership and describes why the Horizons program is an example of a relational leadership development program. The second section describes results from pre- and post-data that assess the extent to which participants in Horizons programs in two states acquired new knowledge about poverty, ways of reducing poverty and leadership skills. The third section describes two case studies on Horizons implementation in Montana and Minnesota. These case studies provide examples from communities participating in the Horizons program that indicate how personnel, community context, and the interaction between personnel and context help to explain the variation in experiences of Horizons communities in the two states. The fourth section describes the broad findings from these case studies and discusses the implications of these findings for other community change programs.

The relational turn in leadership studies

Relational conceptions of leadership focus on the interstitial areas between leaders and followers with special emphasis on interconnectedness and co-evolution (Bradbury & Lichtenstein, 2000; Ospina & Foldy, 2010). Another approach to relational leadership posits that relationships between individuals and organizations are constructed as part of a process and are embedded in a broader societal system (Ospina & Foldy, 2010). Most important for purposes of this article, this approach, known as the constructionist approach, argues that the function of leadership in communities is to take joint action (Uhl-Bien, 2006).

Some consider relational leadership as a trend that has developed because of the increasingly fragmented nature of power (Crosby & Bryson, 2005) and stress the need for new types of integrated leadership approaches privileging collaborative and cross-sector relationships that facilitate community problem-solving and citizen engagement (Bryson, Crosby & Stone, 2006; Huxham & Vangen, 2000). These scholars see civic engagement as a means to an end. In other words, participatory processes and community problem-solving initiatives shape leadership by bringing a more diverse set of voices into the framing of common purposes and creating a more fluid relationship between leaders and followers.

In contrast, others focus on leadership as a process that shapes the relationships between leaders and followers (Drath, 2001; Uhl-Bien, 2006). Rather than focus on the circumstances that produce different interpersonal dynamics related to leadership, these scholars conceptualize leadership as the meaning-making that occurs within groups as various members set a direction and face inevitable adaptive challenges (Drath, 2001; Ospina & Foldy, 2010). As such, civic engagement and related dialogue is part and parcel of the leadership process, and are examples and products of meaning-making and direction-setting.

To date, much of the research that uses the relational perspective of leadership as a lens to understand community development has focused on organizational contexts. For example, Ospina and Foldy's (2010) research on social change organizations focused on a sample of small, non-profit organizations that worked on issues ranging from public health to immigration to homelessness. It may be important to develop a separate vein of research that focuses on leadership in communities since leadership research from organizational settings may be inappropriately applied to leadership in community contexts because community leaders typically lack the formal authority and power vested in positional leaders of organizations (Pigg, 1999). Instead, community leaders use interactions with a diverse set of social ties as a source of power (O'Brien & Hassinger, 1992) to create a common purpose and influence community change with this purpose in mind. Synthesizing the work of a leadership theorist (Rost, 1991) and a community development theorist (Wilkinson, 1991), Pigg (1999) argues that community development leadership focuses more on relationships than people, and more on purpose than effectiveness. In other words, it is the process of reaching consensus on a common purpose through a dialogue that strengthens relationships between community residents and allows the improvement of various aspects of community development (e.g. economic development, environmental protection, etc.) that serve the greater well-being of community residents (Barber, 1984; Dewey, 1927; Wilkinson, 1991).

The Horizons program as relational leadership development

The Horizons program is a multi-state leadership development program with the expressed intent of reducing poverty in rural communities. The rationale behind the program is that the combination of increased awareness of poverty, including different conceptions of what poverty is and the causes of poverty, and improved leadership skills in tandem with civic engagement between community members will result in action to address the incidental, operational, and systemic causes of poverty. The design of Horizons was predicated on several ideas: poverty erodes hope in communities; reducing poverty is a responsibility of all community members; communities possess many of the assets needed to address poverty, but often lack the leadership capacity needed to use those assets; and when building leadership capacity communities would benefit from working with an experienced partner (Hoelting, 2010). In defining poverty, Horizons adopts an encompassing view similar to that of Payne (1996) that acknowledges economic as well as non-economic dimensions.

Deployed in Idaho, Iowa, Minnesota, Montana, North Dakota, South Dakota, and Washington State between 2003 and 2010, Horizons included four phases and reached a total of 283 communities. In each state, university Extension programs worked with steering committees in each community to deliver the Horizons program, which consists of four phases: Study Circles, LeadershipPlenty®, the creation of a community vision, and the development of action plans to address poverty.

Patterned from a curriculum developed by the organization Everyday Democracy, Study Circles are focused community dialogues on poverty that are broken into six sessions and cumulatively last approximately 12 h. Community members are trained to facilitate the conversations, which explore different ways of thinking about poverty as well as the causes and consequences of poverty.

Developed by the Pew Partnership for Civic Change, LeadershipPlenty® is a nine module leadership development training that focuses on a variety of skills, such as identifying community assets, resolving conflict, managing group dynamics, running effective meetings, and building strategic partnerships. LeadershipPlenty® uses a train-the-trainer model that incorporates at least three local trainers who deliver the curriculum to a minimum of 20 community members over approximately 40 h. Following the leadership training, steering committees in each community lead a visioning process with a goal to establish a collective vision of a new direction for the community. Steering committees are required to involve at least 15% of community residents in this process. At the conclusion of the visioning process, participants identify two to five priority areas for action to address poverty. Volunteers sign up to lead different areas of these action plans, using a grant of $10,000 from the Northwest Area Foundation.

In each phase of the Horizons program, a community coach plays a prominent role. Recently, several foundations and community development organizations have stressed the potentially pivotal role of community coaches in encouraging sustainable community change. Among other things, the role of community coaches is to push groups that are working on a community issue to see the bigger community picture for a given question or problem; identify potential collaborators; and highlight learning opportunities (Emery, Hubbell, & Polka, 2011). Each community participating in the Horizons program used a community coach as a liaison with Extension, as well as to ensure that each facet of Horizons included multiple perspectives from the community and that the community conversations and visioning continued to focus on poverty alleviation.

Coaches helped communities to understand the expectations of the NWAF and, therefore, ensured that the communities could access funds that were contingent upon reaching various milestones in the Horizons program. For example, achieving a minimum threshold of participation by community members in each program component was a requirement for communities before they could access certain pools of funding. Coaches also helped motivate the steering committee and other community members to move from one stage of Horizons to the next. Thus, the presence of coaches was integral to successful completion of the Horizons program by participating communities.

Because of its emphasis on dialogue, relationships, consensus-building, and an expansive definition of leader that encompasses positional leaders as well as "ordinary" residents, we consider the Horizons program to be an excellent example of community-level relational leadership development. As conceived in the review of leadership literature above, Horizons is a community-level process that constructs meaning (What is poverty?), sets a direction for action (What changes can we make to address the systemic nature of poverty?), and creates commitment for change (What groups of people will work to implement our proposed changes?). Of the components of Horizons, LeadershipPlenty® and its focus on individual skills is least associated with relational leadership. We argue that training community participants in individual leadership skills (working well with groups, convening more effective meetings, managing conflict, etc.) was of secondary importance for the successes in Horizons when compared to the rich dialogues and relationship building that occurred because of the Study Circles and community visioning exercises.

Research methods

A comparative case study approach was used to examine Horizons communities in Minnesota and Montana. A case study research design based on Yin (2002) compared aspects of each case study to highlight the specific approaches used in the communities, the process that communities followed as they went through Horizons, and the significant outcomes within communities. However, statistical relationships were not estimated, and no claims are made that the research results presented are generalizable to other communities.

Prior to presenting case studies pre- and post-evaluation data from Horizons are first analyzed to assess changes in knowledge of poverty and leadership for Horizons participants for respondents in 29 communities in Minnesota (Horizons Phase Two and Three) and in 16 communities in Montana (Horizons Phase Two). Participants in Study Circles and LeadershipPlenty® were asked to rate their understanding of poverty and leadership practices before and after discussions of poverty and leadership trainings. While the original intention was to include all participants in Study Circles and LeadershipPlenty® trainings in the sample, some Horizons communities experienced modest attrition in their participants due to time and other constraints. In all, responses from 1130 Study Circle participants (450 from Montana and 680 from Minnesota) and 763 LeadershipPlenty® participants (307 from Montana and 456 from Minnesota) are evaluated.

Second, two case studies based on data from interviews with key informants, participant observation, focus groups, and a content analysis of documents created during the visioning process of select Horizons communities in Montana and Minnesota were developed to better understand how Horizons was implemented in each state and how the capacities of communities changed as a result of their participation in Horizons. Key informant interviews included Horizon coaches and state-level administrators. These interviews were composed of a series of open-ended questions designed to determine how coaches and administrators conceived of their roles in Horizons, how communities reacted to working with a coach, and the extent to which communities adopted Horizons principles in efforts to address public decision-making (i.e. whether communities "owned" the process or not). Finally, the authors performed a content analysis on vision statements and action plans produced by select Horizons communities to assess how closely communities connected their efforts to reduce poverty.

Results

Pre- and post-test results

Assessments conducted before and after Horizons Study Circles showed that participants improved their knowledge of issues related to poverty substantially in Montana and Minnesota. Figure 1 indicates the average knowledge score of

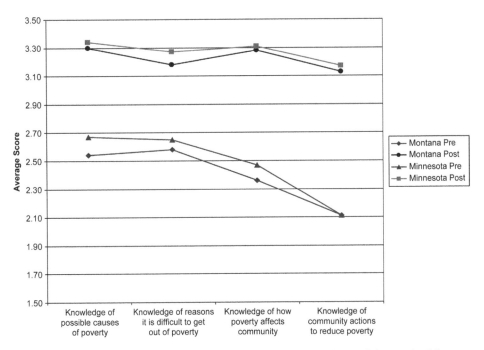

Figure 1. Selected pre- and post-test results for study circle participants in Montana ($n = 450$) and Minnesota ($n = 680$). Note: Scores based on a 4-point scale, with 1 = almost nothing and 4 = a great deal.

participants in Study Circles conducted in Horizons communities in Montana and Minnesota before and after group discussions of poverty (based on a 4-point scale with 1 = almost nothing and 4 = a great deal). The performance and knowledge gains for Study Circle participants in both states were virtually identical. The largest gains in knowledge were in areas related to how poverty affects communities and what community actions can reduce poverty. It is important to note that participants in both states started with relatively low levels of knowledge in these areas.

Figure 2 shows the self-assessments of participants in LeadershipPlenty® on changes in knowledge of leadership issues after their involvement in the program (based on a 5-point scale with 1 = strongly disagree and 5 = strongly agree). Again, the performance of participants in Montana and Minnesota was very similar, with participants in Montana making slightly larger knowledge gains than those in Minnesota. At the same time, participants in both states made notable improvements in their knowledge of various facets of leadership that relational leadership theory suggests are important.

Interviews with key informants revealed that improved knowledge of poverty and leadership were necessary but insufficient conditions for producing community change. Specifically, key informants observed wide variations in the ambitiousness of community action plans and the linkage of these plans to alleviating poverty. They also observed changes in ways that communities engaged in problem solving that did

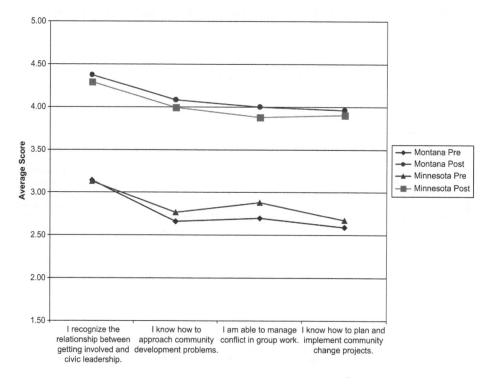

Figure 2.   Selected pre- and post-test results for LeadershipPlenty® Participants in Montana (*n* = 307) and Minnesota (*n* = 456). Note: Scores based on a 5-point scale, with 1 = strongly disagree and 5 = strongly agree.

not necessarily correspond to knowledge gains on the part of Study Circles and LeadershipPlenty® participants. This indicates that the Horizons leadership development curriculum achieved individual empowerment as conceived by Pigg (2002).

Horizons implementation in Montana and Minnesota

The structure and desired outcome of the Horizons program in Montana and Minnesota Extension was similar, however, the programs in the two states differ significantly in terms of implementation and outcome. In Montana, most counties have an Extension office staffed by one or two Extension agents, with each agent offering programming and assistance in multiple areas. For example, depending on the needs of the county and the skills of the agent, an Extension agent may have expertise and work expectation in the areas of agriculture, youth development, family, and consumer sciences or community development. The agents typically work in one county and thus have the opportunity to establish deep connections to the communities in the county through long-term relationships with various stakeholders. This arrangement results in many Montana Extension agents having local knowledge regarding the complex web of social and institutional relationships.

In contrast to Montana's county-based system, Minnesota Extension has adopted a regional system. In this approach, Extension educators (the Minnesota equivalent to an agent) are responsible for establishing relationships and delivering programming and services in multiple counties. This results in the presence of many educators in each regional office, with each educator specializing in a core competency. For example, any given regional Extension office in Minnesota has educators specializing in crops, dairy, youth programs, natural resources, health and nutrition, family resources, livestock, environmental science, community economics, and leadership and civic engagement. The wide variety of expertise among Extension educators in a regional office is possible because of the large scale at which the educators operate. At the same time, the large territory that each regional office covers means that educators necessarily have less time to establish relationships and deliver programming in each county, much less each town, in the region.

This difference in the institutional arrangement of Extension in Montana and Minnesota resulted in important differences in how each state chose to implement Horizons. The most important implementation difference was how each state selected community coaches. Montana Extension elected to use existing county Extension agents as Horizons coaches. This decision meant that county Extension agents served as a coach for a Horizons community if it was located within their county. Typically, coaches in Montana lived in or near the communities where they served as coaches. In contrast, Minnesota Extension chose to hire coaches who had demonstrated expertise in leadership and community development, but were external to existing Extension staff. Newly-hired coaches in Minnesota worked with multiple Horizons communities at any given time, but did not live in any of the communities they served. In each state, coaches helped to establish and then were required to work closely with a steering committee in each community to implement Horizons.

Given these different implementation strategies in Minnesota and Montana, the coaches in each state likely had different strengths and weaknesses. Coaches in Montana tended to have substantial local knowledge about the institutional infrastructure in the community, a strong sense of the community's history, and numerous personal and professional relationships with community members. At the same time, because Extension agents in Montana serve multiple roles within the Extension framework, it was not necessarily the case that each had a strongly developed expertise in general leadership or community development practice. Coaches in Minnesota typically had very little local knowledge about the institutional infrastructure in the community, a weak sense of the community's history, and few personal or professional relationships with community members. In contrast, Minnesota coaches were hired precisely because they had existing expertise in leadership and community development.

In each state, specific community characteristics such as population, poverty rate, and percent of the population involved in the leadership phases of the program are comparable. Tables 1 and 2 illustrate several of these key characteristics in each state.

The outcomes of the program involved both tangible projects that community members described in their respective vision statements and actions plans, as well as more intangible results such as increased networking in the community and trust among community residents. Table 2 illustrates the more significant tangible outcomes from Horizons communities in Montana and Minnesota.

Table 1. Select Horizons communities in Montana and Minnesota illustrating population, poverty rate, and population involved in visioning.

Community	Population (US Census 2000)	Poverty rate (%, US Census 2000)	Population involved in visioning
Montana			
Anaconda	4089	16.0	958
Big timber	1768	11.0	362
Boulder	1445	16.0	241
Brockway	140	18.8	47
Columbus	1931	14.0	295
Crow agency	1552	40.9	271
Culbertson	714	11.0	273
Forsyth	1898	11.0	377
Harlowton	899	10.3	159
Melstone	139	11.2	49
Roundup	1953	20.0	402
Scobey	958	13.0	181
Whitehall	1156	12.0	892
Wibaux	485	10.2	135
Minnesota			
Akeley	412	17.5	93
Appleton	1469	14.7	223
Braham	1276	14.0	194
Chisholm	4764	12.0	747
Elmore	704	12.0	108
Evansville	566	10.0	86
Eveleth	3709	15.0	612
Floodwood	487	19.0	73
Menagha	1220	18.7	192
Moose lake	1185	10.1	241
Pine city	3043	15.0	486
St. James	4500	11.0	726
Starbuck	1314	13.1	202
Waterville	1833	10.6	284

Table 2. Significant outcomes and brief descriptions of example outcomes from Horizons in Montana and Minnesota.

Outcome	Description
Establishment of a community foundation	• Community foundation created to provide funds for needed projects/efforts • Expanded scholarship opportunities
Encourage community cohesion	• Community-wide potlucks to introduce established community of new immigrants • Creation of an "ambassadors" program to welcome newcomers
Housing rehab/ affordable housing	• Secured housing rehab grants • Completed a housing study • Committees formed to co-ordinate volunteers to address housing issues • Partnership formed with national housing organization to begin development of a self-help home ownership program • Provided heaters at no cost for families to reduce heating costs during the winter
Youth programs, early childhood programs, after-school and mentoring activities	• Development of a Head Start Program, after-school program and youth mentoring programs • Town hall meetings organized on underage drinking • Offering youth financial literacy and personal finance classes
Education	• Offering adult basic skills development classes • Educational classes for the family • Creation of "language tables" at local businesses and schools to increase resident's proficiency in Native American languages
Addressing basic/ urgent needs	• Created community food bank in a handicapped-accessible building • Created community garden to help those who need food • Revamping thrift shop
Community clean-ups	• Community clean-up committee formed • Community beautification contest organized

The outcomes in Table 2 illustrate the most popular or significant programs in the communities but this is by no means an exhaustive list. These outcomes document the observable and readily measurable changes in the communities and are attributable to the leadership and civic engagement process.

As the case studies below indicate, coaches played a significant role in the various outcomes of the Horizons program. Though increased knowledge of poverty and improved skills related to leadership were widely experienced by Horizons participants, coaches were an important driver in putting knowledge and skills to use. The effectiveness of coaches partially depended on the interaction between the nature of the coach's connection to the community and the reception each coach received in the community. For example, small, close-knit communities that were less open to outsiders were considerably more receptive to coaches they viewed as already part of their community. On the other hand, in communities that had a less guarded orientation toward outsiders, residents seemed to be more willing to work with outside experts.

Montana Horizons

While Montana Extension worked with 16 communities in Phase II of Horizons, this section examines only two communities. The city of Smelterville[1] is nestled in the Rocky Mountains in southwestern Montana and is the government center for the county. Historically, mining was its primary industry, but with the closing of nearby mines, many jobs and subsequently, much of the tax base was lost. The city is now becoming a recreational center, with top industries being tourism, education, health, and social services. Among the many issues facing the community, approximately 20% of the local housing units are vacant and unemployment is a persistent problem.

The community reluctantly started the Horizons Program after prolonged urging from the community coach who recalled the community's attitude was, "not another community development program!?" The community had tried many programs in the past after the mining jobs were lost and most programs were not successful, so people felt that another program was not going to work now.

As was the case with most of the communities participating in the Horizons program in Montana, the coach lived in the community and was well-respected and served as an Extension agent, with established programs through the local extension office. There was also reluctance according to the coach, because the program "came from the University, and we were tired of being studied to death." The coach reported that she had to talk local leaders and other community members into participating in the program and to form a steering committee. The coach actively sought out and asked members of the community to serve on the steering committee and searched for both key leaders who were known and respected as well as new individuals who had not participated in community planning efforts in the past. According to the coach, "I had to talk leaders into serving on the steering committee, and I had to show them that there would be benefits to participating before they would go along with the program. Their plates were full."

After the Study Circles sessions, the steering committee realized the potential of the program and became more committed and enthused about volunteering time and effort to the program. The coach reports, "The steering committee is now operating independently, and getting so much done, I can hardly keep track of all of the programs and successes." For example, the many action plans that have been initiated include expanded educational opportunities for technical and trade skills training, created new community cleanup opportunities, enhanced afterschool activities for youth, building a volunteer co-ordination network, and a job training program that retrains workers for positions in better-paying jobs.

While it has been difficult to get lower-income individuals to serve on committees and participate in the program, the coach states, "Horizons did raise awareness of poverty in the community. We are much more conscious of being open and inviting and of not alienating those from different income brackets." While income and educational attainment data were not available for this community, according to survey data collected during the leadership training phase of the program, 100% of participants were white even though nearly 4% of community residents were minorities (mostly Native American).

In addition, according to the coach, it was difficult in the past to find even one person to run for some office seats and board positions, but now, "we have too many people running. People are really motivated and we attribute that to Horizons." The coach added "trust was an important factor in getting the community to start and complete the program, and it's an important outcome. There is a lot more trust in the community as a result of Horizons." Trust was enhanced on two levels; first trust between the coach and community members increased because of the relationship formed through Horizons and, second, trust was enhanced between community members through leadership trainings and resulting action planning. The steering committee also continues to meet regularly and is motivated, well-organized, and open to working with new community members.

According to the coach and several steering committee members, relationships and trust were strengthened between the coach and community members and the trust that existed prior to beginning the Horizons program was reported to be absolutely vital in getting initial participation. It is clear that the history of the coach's interaction in the community was a critical asset.

The city of Riverton is located in southeastern Montana situated on the banks of a large river. The city is the government center of the county with education, health, and social services making-up the other major economic drivers in the area. Riverton started as a railroad town when the Northern Pacific Railroad laid tracks across the northern plains. Among the many issues facing the community, nearly 16% of housing units are vacant and 70% of individuals and 45% of households earn less than $30,000. The community enthusiastically embraced the Horizons program and according to the local coach who also serves as the county Extension agent, "negative things had happened in the past, and the community was irritated and looking for opportunities for change. It was fairly easy to get a steering committee together. I just asked people to sign up and they showed up for an initial meeting. It was good timing." While the steering committee was very proactive and "forward thinking" the coach admits that "I shouldn't have done as much as I did. I did a lot of the work myself and should have delegated tasks to the steering committee. They would have been better off if I had let them work through the process more by themselves." The coach did recognize the importance of allowing the community to have ownership of the process and in making community decisions.

Again, trust in the competency of the coach was a factor in assembling the steering committee and getting the community to participate in the program. There was also diversity on the steering committee including an individual involved in local student groups and a local bank administrator who was very influential in the region. This added to the quality of the conversations that took place when the committee met since different stakeholders had different perspectives and interests and would add these perspectives to the discussions.

However, there was not a lot of participation from low income segments of the community even though the steering committee actively tried to recruit members. According to the coach, "we were very cognizant of reaching out to the low income members of our community and tried to be inclusive, but we were not successful." As was true in Smelterville, survey data from program participants in Riverton support this conclusion. The coach did recognize that there is more interaction now among citizens of the community and, by all accounts, the program succeeded in terms of on-the-ground outcomes and more intangible outputs such as improved relationships, communication, and trust in the community.

Among the outcomes of the program, the community started a successful community foundation that continues to raise funds for various community projects and scholarships, an expanded food stamp outreach program, and a town clean-up and beautification program. Perhaps most importantly, the coach states that the community is more engaged, with individuals running for office, more responsive and proactive in talking about community issues, and more people taking part in community actions. Summarizing the program, the coach claims, "this is one of the best things we have ever done." The coach is now playing much less of a role in the initial work-related to the Horizons program. For example, members of the steering committee and other community members are taking the lead on the community foundation planning and outreach efforts and other action committees continue to meet without the coach's involvement.

The coaches from these two examples had an extensive background in community work through Extension, albeit, not necessarily community development work in particular. Examples across the state of coaches with no community development background also resulted in favorable outcomes of community engagement and action plan implementation. It was clear that those coaches, who had developed relationships in the community through successful extension-related programs in the past, were able to implement the Horizons program with favorable outcomes. However, the community development skills and experiences of the coach were not the only critical issue for the success of the Horizons program, but rather success was also contingent on relationships and trust within the community and their experience with collaborative community development efforts in the past.

Minnesota Horizons

While Minnesota Extension worked with 29 communities in Phases II and III of Horizons, this portion of the article examines the relative success of two communities from Phase II. Home to less than 4000 residents, the city of Larkspur's employment base has long focused on resource extraction. The long-term economic decline in the mining industry made poverty a serious problem for Larkspur. At the same time, Larkspur is in a region known for its highly charged political atmosphere and strong streak of independence. This resulted in a high degree of insularity and distrust of outsiders. In the words of the coach that worked with Larkspur, "People only consider you from here if you have multiple generations from here. [When I arrived] they viewed me as an outsider rather than a teammate."

The politically-active nature of residents of Larkspur manifested itself in a Horizons steering group composed of residents extremely passionate about regaining prosperity for Larkspur and politically influential enough to make change a reality. According to the coach, "in some communities you have to suggest making political connections; in Larkspur it is an everyday kind of thing." On one hand, the coalescing of these powerful individuals, many of whom had extensive experience in leadership and community development efforts, signaled that Larkspur was "ready" to work on a community development initiative. The steering committee proved to be decisive, well-organized and confident in their decision-making, resulting in rapid movement on community development initiatives.

On the other hand, it is unclear if Horizons resulted in new perspectives from Larkspur participating in the planning and implementation of community development initiatives. For example, while there is evidence of individuals who have never run for elected public offices starting campaigns at the conclusion of the Horizons program, it appears that these individuals were already part of the informal networks with significant influence on public decision-making. Initially, participants in some of the Horizons programming in Larkspur were individuals who lived well outside of Larkspur, but were relatives of powerful community members. Thus, the dialogues about poverty and leadership training involved residents (and, in some cases, non-residents) who were already relatively powerful and privileged in Larkspur.

Despite the lack of evidence that the public decision-making process has become more open in Larkspur, the town's action plan set forth some ambitious civic engagement projects at the conclusion of Horizons that sought wider participation by residents in the civic life of Larkspur. Examples include the creation of an annual winter carnival, participation in National Night Out block parties, adopt-a-block programs, and a variety of youth programming including skateboard, ice skating, and bicycle events. By all accounts, these initiatives have proven to be remarkably successful, drawing large and diverse audiences of residents. Other programming ideas, such as programs to increase ridership on public transportation and provide funds to assist households with delinquent utility bills, had direct connections to poverty alleviation, but have not been implemented in a widespread or systematic fashion.

The experience of the coach in Larkspur clearly highlights the tension between being "of" the community rather than "outside" of the community. As an outsider to Larkspur, the coach was rarely consulted by the steering committee and usually learned about decisions the committee made regarding their activities several weeks after the fact. As the coach commented, "It was like they wanted access to the resources [from Horizons] without the oversight that came with those resources." While this indicates a high level of ownership of the Horizons program in Larkspur, the lack of communication between the coach and the steering committee did not allow the coach opportunities to push the committee to be more inclusive and involve residents from outside the existing power structure in an authentic way. At the same time, widespread participation by residents in civic programs suggests that the town may have taken steps to lay the ground work for a more inclusive future.

With a population just under 5000 people, the city of Yarrow's economic base is considerably more diverse than Larkspur's. Still, much of the economy is dominated by relatively low-paying jobs in meat processing and the service sector. Recently, a large immigrant population composed primarily of Latinos and Somalis has moved to Yarrow to take advantage of job openings in the meat processing plant. While it is certainly not limited to the immigrant population of Yarrow, poverty has been a particular problem for this group. Thus, with the mandate of Horizons to foster leadership to reduce poverty in mind, the immigrant population was an important group to include in the Horizons process in Yarrow.

Similar to Larkspur, the Horizons program in Yarrow initially had a tenuous relationship with its coach. With a background in local politics and community organizing, the coach in Yarrow immediately pressed for broad participation and a reshuffling of the power structure in Yarrow in initial meetings with the steering committee. This created friction because the steering committee did not represent a diverse set of views and was composed of relatively powerful residents. Over time, the coach figured out how to push the steering committee members in less overt ways to open the process to a more diverse set of voices. In the coach's words, "In Yarrow I had to go in and really dig around for broader engagement [so that] we could talk about poverty in a more genuine way ... where [the steering committee] learned the most was how to engage people without being patronizing and talking about poverty in a way that everyone can hear."

The coach's efforts to broaden participation in Horizons paid off. Horizons in Yarrow experienced a surge in involvement by youth and immigrants. In fact, after realizing that the Study Circles aspect of Horizons would not attract enough Latino residents to satisfy minimum thresholds outlined by NWAF, the steering committee and coach elected to extend their timeline for the Study Circle exercises and make a concerted effort to discover the informal leadership in the Latino community and offer bilingual trainings for facilitators. Ultimately, almost one-fifth of Study Circle participants and one-third of LeadershipPlenty® participants in Yarrow were Latino.

While Yarrow was relatively less insular than Larkspur, working with the community as an outsider was a challenge for the coach. When asked about the reception in Yarrow, the coach responded, "There was lots of welcoming language, like 'we're so lucky to have your help,' but there was a shallow bottom to our interactions. Like most places, Yarrow has a very complex system of social dynamics and the rules of [those dynamics] were tightly held." Learning the rules that governed social dynamics in Yarrow and establishing trust with the steering committee and other members of the community took time and certainly contributed to early missteps in community interactions on the part of the coach. At the same time, lacking a base of local knowledge in Yarrow and being treated as an outsider was not without its benefits. As the coach noted, "It was always clear that I was an outsider, so I never took [reproaches by community members] personally, but people were also more likely to be honest with me. It's like you tell a therapist or bartender all kinds of things because they don't have anything to do with [your problems]."

With a diverse set of voices involved in the Horizons process, the action plan created at the community visioning event focused on poverty alleviation and improving the lives of poor, immigrant households living in Yarrow. Specifically, the action plan called for the creation of adult ESL and financial literacy classes; a bilingual certified nursing assistant training program; a bilingual day care worker training program; the construction of bus shelters at transit and school bus stops; and publishing a resource directory that is inclusive and available to all residents. In a sign that the processes advocated by Horizons have become institutionalized in Yarrow, the action plan also called for a new round of Study Circles focused on race relations to help reduce racial tensions between Anglo and Latino residents.

Despite the lack of local knowledge and initial trouble navigating a relatively insular community, the coach in Yarrow helped the community use the Horizons program to learn how to engage a diverse set of residents, identify community problems, and build consensus around solutions to these problems. While poverty is still a pressing problem for many Yarrow residents, the community has taken steps to address the challenges that many of these residents face. Perhaps most impressive, there seems to be anecdotal evidence that the well-being of different groups of Yarrow residents are inextricably linked together.

Discussion and conclusion

Given the pervasive and, in some cases, multi-generational nature of rural poverty in Horizons communities, program participants had the difficult task of reducing poverty through leadership development. At the same time, the evidence presented in this article indicates that Horizons had the potential to profoundly affect a community's sense of identity and fundamentally change residents' willingness to become engaged in their communities and work together to make improvements. The most widespread effects of Horizons on empowerment seem to have been at the individual level. Unambiguously, participants in Study Circles and Leadership-Plenty® trainings learned more about the causes and consequences of poverty as well as leadership skills that encourage collective action. Evidence presented in the case studies of this article also indicates that Horizons changed how communities conceived of leadership and approached problem-solving, but that the degree of change was uneven among communities.

We suggest that different methods of Horizons implementation adopted by states (i.e. a community versus regionally-based coach approach) may explain some of the variation in community capacity, because these implementation methods indirectly influenced the types of skills and knowledge possessed by coaches and the reception that these coaches received in the communities they served. Coaches play a significant role in the delivery of the Horizons program and were often key figures in helping community residents organize for change.

For example, in the case of Montana, coaches were not necessarily experts in leadership or community engagement but often had strong professional and personal connections with many community residents. Residents of Montana communities were quick to embrace their coaches and, as the example of Smelterville above indicates, coaches used their established trust with community members to jump start reluctant residents and infuse energy into the process. The deep connections coaches had with communities in Montana sometimes impeded the transfer of ownership of the Horizons program. For example, in Riverton the coach was so wrapped up in the work and recognized in hindsight that efforts slowed the rate at which residents assumed the bulk of the organizing responsibilities in the Horizons work. In neither example in Montana were the coaches or steering committees able to attract many low income residents to participate in the program. However, a new cadre of leaders did come forward who had not participated previously in community planning or action.

In contrast, in Minnesota coaches typically had specific expertise in leadership development, but rarely had a wide network of personal or professional contacts in their communities. This resulted in community residents having to overcome distrust of the coach in order to fully benefit from the coach's expertise and insights. In the case of Larkspur, the distrust of the coach never dissipated and the coach did not have the opportunity to push the steering group to expand participation in the Horizons activities and embrace the model of relational leadership espoused by the NWAF. On the other hand, in Yarrow the community did overcome this initial distrust and benefited significantly from the talents of the coach. Consequently, the steering committee learned new ways to identify informal leaders from the immigrant community and dramatically expanded participation in Horizons.

We note the characteristics of personnel involved in implementing leadership development programs, which are potentially influenced by program implementation strategies, and community context are important in determining how communities change after participating in a leadership development program. Specifically, the different experiences of coaches in Montana and Minnesota suggests that if a community change strategy uses coaching techniques, the characteristics of a coach are important. If getting a community change program off of the ground is the main challenge, it may be wise to select a coach with ample local knowledge and a well-developed social network who can encourage initial participation. One pitfall with this approach is the potential for community involvement to stall and remain confined to individuals within established networks.

Another pitfall is increased difficulty transferring ownership of the community change process out of the hands of the coach and to a wider group that is representative of the community. Selecting a coach who will be viewed as an outsider in the community may improve the chances of wider community involvement (since this coach may have to recruit participants without relying on social networks) and a smoother transfer of ownership of the community change process to the community (since the coach will not be viewed as a community member who should participate). At the same time, it may be considerably more difficult for an outsider coach to gain the confidence of community members that is already in place for insider coaches.

Perhaps the most important finding from this research is that relatively minor investments in leadership development can yield dramatic changes in a community's capacity to identify and address problems. In many instances in Montana and Minnesota, wide swaths of community members who had either failed to recognize that poverty existed in their community or only understood poverty as an economic concept gained a deeper appreciation for the causes and consequences of poverty and ways of reducing it. Further, residents in many communities report that they now recognize the importance of community networking and new relationships and feel a renewed sense of hope and pride in their communities. Poverty still exists in Horizons communities and the vagaries of market forces and policy decisions made at other jurisdictional levels will continue to influence the depth and breadth of economic poverty in the communities. At the same time, residents of Horizons communities have developed skills and insights that will allow them to conceive of and implement initiatives that address the myriad forms of poverty.

While the Horizons program addressed poverty, it is not difficult to imagine how similar techniques (Study Circles, LeadershipPlenty®, community visioning, and developing an action plan) could be tailored to focus on a variety of issues that affect small, rural communities. Focusing on community assets and participatory processes generates new ideas about how to frame and solve a community problem. Because the Horizon's approach is inherently relational it also enhances social capital within the community that has many positive externalities, such as increasing the community's ability to cope with current and future problems.

Note

1. Smelterville is a pseudonym. We also provide pseudonyms for the three other communities described in this article.

References

Barber, B.R. (1984). *Strong democracy: Participatory politics for a new age*. Berkeley, CA: University of California Press.

Bradbury, H. & Lichtenstein, B. (2000). Relationality in organizational research: Exploring the 'space between'. *Organizational Science, 11*, 551–564.

Bryson, J., Crosby, B., & Stone, M. (2006). Design and implementation of cross-sector collaborations: Propositions from the literature. *Public Administration Review, 66*(1), 44–55.

Crosby, B. & Bryson, J. (2005). *New leadership for the common good*. San Francisco, CA: Jossey-Bass.

Dewey, J. (1927). *The public and its problems*. Athens, OH: Swallow Press.

Drath, W.H. (2001). *The deep blue sea: Rethinking the source of leadership*. San Francisco, CA: Jossey-Bass.

Emery, M., Hubbell, K. & Polka, B. (2011). *A field guide to community coaching*. Retrieved from www.communitycoaching.com.

Erickson, D., Reid, C., Nelson, L., O'Shaughnessy, A., & Berube, A. (2008). *The enduring challenge of concentrated poverty in America*. The Federal Reserve System and the Brookings Institution. Retrieved from http://www.brookings.edu/reports/2008/1024_concentrated_poverty.aspx.

Hoelting, J. (2010). Horizons program mobilizes communities to address rural poverty. *Community Dividend*, April, Federal Reserve Bank of Minneapolis.

Holliday, A.L. & Dwyer, R.E. (2009). Suburban neighborhood poverty in U.S. metropolitan areas in 2000. *City & Community*, *8*, 155–176.

Huxham, C. & Vangen, S. (2000). Leadership in the shaping and implementation of collaboration agendas: How things happen in a (not quite) joined-up world. *The Academy of Management Journal*, *43*, 1159–1175.

Jargowsky, P.A. (1997). *Poverty and place: Ghettos, barrios, and the American city*. New York: Russell Sage Foundation.

Kretzmann, J.P. & McKnight, J.L. (1993). *Building communities from the inside out: A path toward finding and mobilizing a community's assets*. Evanston, IL: Institute for Policy Research, Northwestern University.

O'Brien, D. & Hassinger, E. (1992). Community attachment among leaders in five rural communities. *Rural Sociology*, *57*, 521–534.

Ospina, S. & Foldy, E. (2010). Building bridges from the margins: The work of leadership in social change organizations. *The Leadership Quarterly*, *21*, 292–307.

Payne, R.K. (1996). *A framework for understanding poverty*. Highlands, TX: aha! Process, Inc.

Pigg, K.E. (1999). Community leadership and community theory: A practical synthesis. *Journal of the Community Development Society*, *30*, 196–212.

Pigg, K.E. (2002). Three faces of empowerment: Expanding the theory of empowerment in community development. *Journal of the Community Development Society*, *33*(1), 107–123.

Rost, J.D. (1991). *Leadership for the twenty-first century*. Westport, CT: Praeger.

Uhl-Bien, M. (2006). Relational leadership theory: Exploring the social processes of leadership and organizing. *The Leadership Quarterly*, *17*, 654–676.

Weber, B., Jensen, L., Miller, K., Mosley, J., & Fisher, M. (2005). A critical review of rural poverty literature: Is there truly a rural effect? *International Regional Science Review*, *28*, 381–414.

Wilkinson, K.P. (1991). *The community in rural America*. New York: Greenwood Press.

Yin, R.K. (2002). *Case study research: Design and methods* (3rd ed.). Thousand Oaks, CA: Sage Publications.

Lessons from the field: mapping Saskatchewan's Pipeline of Entrepreneurs and Enterprises in order to build a provincial operating system for entrepreneurship

Gregg Lichtenstein[a] and Thomas S. Lyons[b]

[a]Collaborative Strategies, USA; [b]Department of Management, Zicklin School of Business, Baruch College, City University of New York, NY, USA

This article describes the initial stages of a long-term change project, to implement a province-wide entrepreneurial development system in Saskatchewan, Canada. The project used a highly participative planning process to engage 300 stakeholders in a new method to meaningfully segment the marketplace of entrepreneurs and enterprises in a community or region. This process, referred to as the Pipeline of Entrepreneurs and Enterprises, guides economic development investments and moves them from a piece-meal approach of addressing entrepreneurial needs to one that is more systemic.

Introduction

In 2006, the authors developed a new framework, called the Pipeline of Entrepreneurs and Enterprises (the Pipeline), for meaningfully segmenting the marketplace of entrepreneurs and enterprises in a community or region to support growth and development (Lichtenstein and Lyons, 2006, 2010). The Pipeline helps community and regional leaders answer fundamental questions about who these entrepreneurs are, what they need, and how they can best be helped to build successful companies. The Pipeline refocuses economic development strategies to

---

The project described in this article had its origins in a paper by the authors published in the Special Issue on Entrepreneurship in Community Development for the Journal of the Community Development Society (Volume 35, No. 1, 2004). That article was entitled "Building Entrepreneurial Communities: The Appropriate Role of Enterprise Development Activities" (by Lichtenstein et al., 2004). Later that year, one of the authors was contacted by Brad Wall, The Leader of the Official Opposition Saskatchewan Party (Canada), who requested permission to quote from that paper in an economic vision statement he was preparing for public release, specifically referencing the concept of taking a "systematic approach to enterprise and community development efforts by creating a community-wide entrepreneurial development system." In 2007, Mr. Wall was elected Premier of the Province and gradually began to implement an economic development agenda based in part on several of the key principles articulated in that paper (Wall, 2004).

assist entrepreneurs in a highly targeted, systemic, and systematic way. Communities are enabled to manage their economies as a portfolio of business assets, allowing them to compete more strategically in the global economy.

In 2010, Enterprise Saskatchewan, the provincial agency responsible for economic development, engaged one of the authors to map Saskatchewan's Pipeline of Entrepreneurs and Enterprises. The purpose of this project was to create a framework and an analytical segmentation of the Province's entrepreneurship marketplace to be used to guide its economic development investments and improve the system for entrepreneurial development in the province. This article describes that project and its impacts.

Two things make this project unusual and worthy of examination. First is the use of an innovative tool (the Pipeline of Entrepreneurs and Enterprises, which is discussed later) to frame the analysis process, and make it actionable in a very grounded manner. The mapping of local communities was conducted on a geographical (13 regions), demographic (according to populations of youth, Aboriginal, and immigrants), and industrial (i.e. sector) basis and was aggregated to create a macro-level Pipeline for the Province. This method of mapping along multiple dimensions and in a distributed and disaggregated manner allows decision makers to examine the parts (micro or individual communities), the whole (the entire Province) and the inter-relations of the parts to the whole.

The second unique element is the planning process by which the economic development strategies to increase the volume and improve the flow of entrepreneurs and enterprises in the Pipeline were selected. The planning and design process directly engaged over 300 different stakeholders (e.g. entrepreneurs, service providers, community leaders, and public officials) in both a bottom up and top down manner. The process not only involved making decisions about investments in individual communities and their micro-level pipelines, but also about how those various individual pipelines must be integrated to insure the economic health and well-being of the entire Province, not just selected elements of it. This project directly confronts the challenges to using a participatory planning process to capture the wisdom of the whole while being systemic as well as strategic in designing more effective economic development solutions.

Theoretical support

This project has its theoretical and conceptual roots in the literatures of the related fields of community development, economics, economic development, entrepreneurship, sociology, and urban/regional planning. The project sought to foster community economic development through the facilitation of successful entrepreneurship among residents (an effort known as community enterprise development). The goal was to enhance quality of life throughout the Province, and within its specific geographical, political and demographic communities, by creating wealth via the development of business assets. Accomplishing this goal rests on the premise that this asset development must be done by creating a system that permits a rational, synoptic approach and that links the major actors – entrepreneurs, entrepreneurship service organizations, other business people, government agencies, and policy makers – together to build and sustain this system.

Mark Granovetter (1985) offers a useful way of thinking about an endeavor such as this when he urges a balance between "agency" and "structure." This approach blends the individual's impact on his context or community and the community's impact on the individual. The key is to not over-emphasize individualism or collectivism. In this case, the entrepreneur represents the individual, who must have room to innovate and pursue individual wealth in building a business asset. However, as Fortunato and Alter (2011) have observed, the entrepreneur is more likely to pursue his opportunity when a system of support provided by the community exists. All of this suggests that the relationship between entrepreneur and community must be symbiotic, but does the entrepreneur actually contribute?

It has been widely acknowledged that economic development can create more diverse, stronger and healthier communities (Cypher & Dietz, 2009; Lichtenstein & Lyons, 2010). Conversely, a lack of economic development can be deleterious to the most basic standard of living (Arrow et al., 1995). Economic development takes the assets developed by the community and mobilizes them (Phillips & Pittman, 2009). Entrepreneurial start-up businesses – the community's business assets – have been shown to have the greatest impact on a community's economic development in terms of growth and job creation (Birch, 1979; Carree & Thurik, 2010). Thus, entrepreneurs, through their pursuit of opportunity and individual wealth creation, contribute to the wealth and well-being of communities. Taken collectively, the impact of the activities of all of a community's entrepreneurs can be economically transformative (Lichtenstein & Lyons, 2001). Porter and Kramer (2011) refer to this coming together of the interests of business and of society as "shared value."

However, as Phillips and Pittman (2009) have suggested, this must be true economic *development* and not merely economic growth, which are not the same thing. Growth is scalar – it focuses on quantity. Development is qualitative. It strives for better, not just more. This is an important insight for economic developers from the community perspective, but it is also important to fostering entrepreneurship. The goal in the case of the Saskatchewan project is not merely to generate more entrepreneurs, but to develop better entrepreneurs. This is reflected in the Pipeline of Entrepreneurs and Enterprises model being used there, which segments entrepreneurs by their skill level and their enterprises by their stage in the business life cycle (a developmental process).

What can communities do to develop a high quality Pipeline of Entrepreneurial activity? Porter (2000) argues that entrepreneurs are attracted to places that offer a cluster of business services. Levine (1997), writing about financial services, notes that having a system of support in place before the entrepreneur begins the pursuit of her opportunity is important. This enterprise development system must be complete, in terms of the services offered, and well networked (Loveridge, 2007).

Effective enterprise development must be intentional – it must be planned (Ciegis & Gineitiene, 2008). It must be the result of a multi-tiered, interactive process that involves all the relevant players in the community. This builds trust, social capital, and institutional capacity (Fisher, Geenen, Jurcevic, McClintock, & Davis, 2009; Varol, Eroskum, & Gurer, 2011). This process also needs to have a clear structure (Phillips & Pittman, 2009). Drawing from the asset-based community development model and its focus on asset mapping as applied to enterprise development (Kretzmann & McKnight, 1996; Markley, Macke, & Luther, 2005), the Pipeline of Entrepreneurs and Enterprises affords such a structure.

This project has also been influenced by the diverse literature on systems (Ackoff, 1981; Ackoff & Emery, 1972; Beer, 1985; Dunn, 1974; Katsenelinboigen, 1984). Its goal has been to intentionally develop or manage a system – defined as a condition where the whole is greater than the sum of the parts. In too many parts of our society and world, the whole is often much less than the sum of the parts; a situation that leaves considerable potential for positive impact on the table.

Framing the intervention

The starting point: a pipeline analysis

Entrepreneurs are people who create wealth by capturing market opportunities and converting them into business assets; they are the "engines" of economic development in a community. We prize large companies, but all large companies were once small companies started by entrepreneurs. An entrepreneurial economy requires entrepreneurs.

The critical measure of an economy's vitality is the quantity and quality of its entrepreneurs and how well they are matched to the market opportunities pursued. Since it is indeed possible to develop entrepreneurs, the supply is not fixed. Our society methodically cultivates many other kinds of talent; why not entrepreneurs (Lichtenstein and Lyons, 2001)?

Entrepreneurship must be both encouraged and supported, but in strategic ways. Entrepreneurs are not all the same; they have differing needs. This project used a new approach to mapping and analyzing the business assets in a community or region, known as the Pipeline of Entrepreneurs and Enterprises. The image of a pipeline calls to mind the idea of a conduit or the concept of deal flow in the sense used by venture capitalists, bankers or even salespeople. It represents the quantity and quality of the entrepreneurs and enterprises in specific area.

The Pipeline uses three dimensions to map the community's entrepreneurs and enterprises:

(1) The vertical dimension represents the rungs in the skill ladder and sorts entrepreneurs into five skill levels: Rookies, Single A's, Double A's, Triple A's, and Major Leaguers.
(2) The horizontal dimension represents the six life cycle stages of the business: pre-venture, existence, early growth, expansion, maturity, and decline.
(3) The depth dimension (or the number within the cells in the two-dimensional graphic below or the height of the bar in the three-dimensional graphic) represents the quantity of entrepreneurs and enterprise in a community or region that occupy a particular segment of the Pipeline (Figure 1).

Transforming an economy requires focusing on both volume and flow of the Pipeline. The two goals in successfully managing the Pipeline are to increase the quantity (the volume) of the supply of entrepreneurs and enterprises in the community and to improve their quality (the flow); in other words, to help the Pipeline grow and flow. There are places where the flow tends to slow, stop or terminate. These are caused by mismatches between the entrepreneur's, or entrepreneurial team's, skills and the life cycle stage of the enterprise. Moving a business from one stage to the next requires structural changes that can only be made by an entrepreneur with an appropriate skill-set. By increasing the flow and avoiding these stress points, the "quality" of the entrepreneurs and enterprises in a community's portfolio of business assets improves (Lichtenstein and Lyons, 2010).

Two variables describe the "quality" of the entrepreneurs and enterprises. Skill level represents the quality of the entrepreneurs. Stage in the life cycle of the business

LIFE CYCLE STAGES

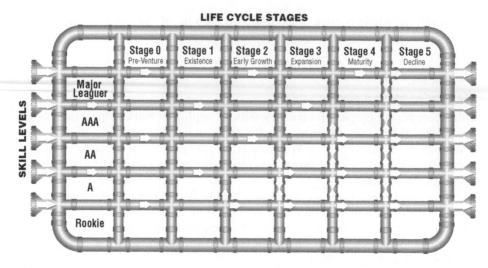

Figure 1.   The Pipeline of Entrepreneurs and Enterprises. © Collaborative Strategies LLC, 2010.

captures the quality of the business. The ideal flow of the Pipeline is always from the lower left (lower skill levels and earlier life cycle stages) to the upper right (higher skill levels and later life cycle stages in the business) (Lichtenstein and Lyons, 2010).

Flow in the Pipeline is not smooth and linear; there are graduated, discontinuous intervals that the entrepreneur and the enterprise must traverse. It is crucial to understand that *movement from one segment of the Pipeline to another requires a transformation* – either the development of new skills by the entrepreneur or a change in the structure of the business that permits movement to the next stage in the life cycle. This key principle captures (or operationalizes) the fundamental difference between growth and development. Growth is a scalar concept that describes linear changes within a particular structure, like increase in sales, etc. Development represents a fundamental change in structure – either within the thinking and skills of the entrepreneur or within the operations of a business (Lichtenstein and Lyons, 2010).

Utilizing the Pipeline of Entrepreneurs and Enterprises as a framework and a tool enables users to take a more systemic approach to economic development. It provides the discipline to make an entrepreneurial development system practical, operational and grounded in the specific needs of the entrepreneurs of that community or region.

Community change intervention

The questions this project was designed to address include: what is the potential of such a system for the Province of Saskatchewan and what will it take to realize or capture that potential?

The concept of systems is the key differentiating factor here. Like most places around the world, Saskatchewan (in collaboration with the Canadian National Government) had taken a piece-meal approach to addressing entrepreneurial needs:

when a clear problem was identified (e.g. a lack of technical assistance), a program was designed and launched to address it. This led to the creation of a variety of "point" solutions, but collectively they did not constitute a system.

For example, with respect to the enterprise development service providers, while the depth and breadth of the assistance available to entrepreneurs in the Province is impressive, when looked at overall and from the perspective of the whole, the situation is "disorganized." In summary:

- Entrepreneurs (current and prospective) are uncertain where to go for assistance and are vocal about this issue.
- It is unclear in which areas and subjects service providers specialize and excel; and
- Public sector funders are challenged about how to allocate scarce resources among the numerous program requests for support.

There is enormous potential for major increases in efficiency and effectiveness as well as scale and sustainability in the ability to meet the needs of provincial entrepreneurs, if a system could be forged out of the parts. This was part of the Province's vision (as represented by the Premier and Enterprise Saskatchewan) – a way for a rural province, a little more than one million in population scattered over a territory three times the size of the state of Texas, with limited financial resources to establish a competitive advantage in economic development against larger rivals with more resources.

The project involved the following activities:

- Initial presentations to stakeholders and constituencies to build an under-standing of the project's purposes and support: entrepreneurs, public-sector, non-profit and private sector service providers, individuals from three different divisions with Enterprise Saskatchewan as well as other ministries in the provincial government.
- Direct interviews with 193 entrepreneurs from a geographically, demographi-cally and industrially diverse and representative set of participants (whose skills and life cycle stages were assessed for their fit into the Pipeline). This information was used to generate maps of the Pipeline of Entrepreneurs for the province as a whole as well as the other 18 micro-Pipelines (for 13 geographical regions, three demographic groups and two market sectors).
- Interviews with more than 100 enterprise development service providers to determine the segment in the Pipeline in which they work.
- Interviews with 22 key informants – individuals who have broad exposure and interact regularly with the business community, such as successful entrepreneurs, key bankers, investors, public, and private (e.g. accountants, lawyers, etc.) business service providers as well as industry and demographic sector specialists to get their "take" on the entrepreneurship activities within the Province.
- A Strategy Faire involving more than 75 participants, include 38 individuals who served as champions for the 19 Pipelines developed for this project. The strategy faire was a day-long, highly interactive event designed to collect information/intelligence about the activities in the individual Pipelines, and to generate actionable ideas, options and recommendations improve the quality and increasing the quantity of entrepreneurs in all 19 Pipelines.

- A review and analysis of the available secondary data on entrepreneurs and businesses within the province (e.g. number of businesses and their sizes, business starts and closures, etc.) and other economic studies.
- On-going meetings with a client Steering Committee comprising nine representatives of Enterprise Saskatchewan to educate them about the process and jointly make decisions.

Individual outcomes

This project focused on achieving five outcomes:

Generating actionable recommendations for systems-level changes that will build a Provincial Operating System for entrepreneurship

The first challenge was to create and maintain a systems perspective or frame for all of the participants, meaning a focus on the whole rather than the parts. Each participant tended to view themselves as individual actors operating in isolation. Their attention was shifted by asking them to see themselves as a part of a larger whole. These framing activities were undertaken in the initial presentations about the project to the various stakeholder groups, in the individual interview questions and discussions, at the Strategy Faire and in the final presentations or conversations.

Focusing on the whole enabled facilitators to significantly alter and re-organize stakeholder perspectives on many issues commonly faced. For example, one complaint by entrepreneurs in the Province (which, in past experience, is echoed by entrepreneurs almost everywhere in the world) is the difficulty they have in finding the right service provider from among the plethora of organizations that work in this field. Rather than taking this criticism personally or experiencing it as an attempt to assign blame to an individual service provider, a systems frame helped each to see that this was a universal problem from which no one was exempt – meaning that this was a property of the system as a whole. Matching entrepreneurs to service providers is currently sub-optimal because no system exists for doing it in an efficient and effective manner.

A systems frame helped the participants understand that this is not a problem that can be solved by any one of the individual service providers. This problem will never be solved unless the accountability and responsibility for doing so is placed at the appropriate level. The discussion then more easily moved to an exploration of where this responsibility belongs and what the requirements are for a successful solution.

This was just one example of the many systemic problems examined during this project, problems that were familiar to every one of the stakeholders but had proven to be intractable to solution by each one acting individually (to the continued frustration of everyone). By holding a systems frame, the facilitators were able to transform issues whose causes as well as solutions were not understandable, into problems that were suddenly clear and more actionable.

This change in dynamics is achieved in large part by reducing the anxiety and resistance that accompanies discussions of lower-dimensionality where the parts of a system are aligned against each other in a zero-sum competition. By expanding the participants' perspective and looking at the larger context or system in which everyone operates, the emotions that tend to block an open exploration are not invoked; rather, they can be put aside, temporarily at least. This phase of the process can be freed, in some measure, of the usual politics.

A systems frame also enables all of the stakeholders to draw upon and use their collective wisdom in a much more powerful way. Participants were encouraged to view their issues from multiple perspectives and to see how two seemingly irreconcilable observations can both be true. For example, in one project conducted by the authors, entrepreneurs split evenly on the answer to a question about the availability of financing for their ventures. We could not make sense of it (how could both sets of observations be true?), until we sorted the entrepreneurs according to their positions in the Pipeline. That distribution revealed that entrepreneurs in the upper right hand corner of the Pipeline (from the Double A skill level up and from the Expansion Stage in the life cycle on), found that there was more than enough financing in the region to fund their ventures.

By contrast, all entrepreneurs in the lower left hand corner of the Pipeline (from the Single A skill level down and from the Pre-Venture through Early Growth Stages), reported that there is no money available in this region for their ventures. Both observations were correct, but their truth depended on which their location in the Pipeline. The conflict could only be productively resolved through a much deeper and fine-grained examination of the issue (Lichtenstein and Lyons, 2010).[1]

The purpose of creating a systems frame is to generate actionable recommendations for systems-level changes. A reasonable question to ask at this point is what kind of recommendation qualifies? A comment made by a key informant during this project offers a perfect example. This person argued that by insuring the successful transition of ownership from the current generation of entrepreneurs to the next generation of entrepreneurs, the province will naturally create a class of angel investors (from among the ranks of the senior generation). He correctly observed that the two, seemingly separate issues (of succession and lack of access to capital by entrepreneurs) are closely linked – an observation that silo oriented (non-systemic) thinkers overlook. He was suggesting that the way to create the result that everyone wants in the financial arena is not to look at solving the problem directly, say by providing tax credits, but rather by looking at the larger context in which these issues are embedded. Success in one area – succession – will create leverage or a domino effect in another area of the system because of their natural interconnections. Creating or facilitating such linkages, known as "virtuous cycles," is the key to successfully designing and managing systems. This then, constitutes an effective recommendation for a systems-level change.

Another example comes from a member of the Steering Committee, who reported on an 'a-ha' moment that occurred during a discussion about how to design a single point of entry 'in-take system' for matching entrepreneurs to service providers. "The 'a-ha' was (based on) realizing that by adding this one component to the system, if done correctly, we could address multiple concerns. Specifically, the service provision maze would be simplified by triaging demand and continuous feedback from the referral system. Entrepreneurs would have a simplified, single-point of engagement that would be a neutral and trustworthy source of direction. Governance would be improved by the information that could be collected directly from entrepreneurs. Gaps in support and changes in the needs of entrepreneurs would, presumably, be well documented through continuous engagement with the in-take system."[2]

Creating and maintaining a systems frame that can produce these types of ideas and recommendations is not easy to do. It requires continuous attention and skilled facilitation by someone familiar with the substantive issues faced by the participants. Such domain-specific knowledge provided the facilitators sufficient credibility with participants to encourage them to suspend judgment and join in a different way of looking at the issues.

There is a major difference between being able to recognize the importance or value of systems thinking and being able to use it to produce system change. The latter activity demands a level of skill that cannot be achieved merely by exposure. The expectation was that over time, a sufficient number of participants would develop the skills necessary to engage in such thinking and behavior by themselves; that goal was clearly beyond the scope of a five-month project. However, just how much change would be required in order to do this became clear from the following incident.

The afternoon of the Strategy Faire was devoted to a plenary discussion on how to design an integrated operating system for entrepreneurship out of the variety of independent programs that already exist in the province. Surprisingly, the participants could not engage in that discussion, even after having successfully participated in a half-day interactive session where they had been asked to behave as a system and generate system-level recommendations. With the right structure and support, they could perform the work, but did not yet have a sufficient quantity of experiences and the necessary skills to step back and critically reflect about them in an abstract way. This demonstrated the critical importance of creating and maintaining a systems perspective or frame for all of the participants. The need to develop the capacity to produce and maintain this systems frame on their own became a major recommendation.

Producing recommendations grounded in the needs of the marketplace of entrepreneurs, as represented by the Pipeline of Entrepreneurs and Enterprises

Economic development investments are frequently sold on the basis of the faddishness of the solution, political expediency, or the persuasiveness of salesmanship of the champion, rather than on the basis of a rigorous assessment of the needs in the marketplace (Dewar, 1998). Instilling a customer-driven discipline insures that the needs of entrepreneurs are at the center of all investment decisions.

This discipline was achieved through the introduction and use of the Pipeline of Entrepreneurs and Enterprises as a tool for segmenting the marketplace. The Pipeline was used to map the population of entrepreneurs for the Province as a whole and for 18 constituent parts. The Pipeline was also used in all recommendations. For example, one goal of the Strategy Faire was to generate ideas or "deals" for investment in the various Pipelines that would address particular weaknesses. All deals had to first specify the customers for the investment – which part of the Pipeline of Entrepreneurs and Enterprises (i.e. skill level and business life cycle stage) is targeted. Second, the deal sheets had to include a description of the needs of that specific market segment (based on input from actual entrepreneurs, not simply a service provider's representation of those needs), before proposing a solution.

The need for precision in specifying the particular Pipeline segment target is due to the fact that a single investment will not be effective for multiple segments of the Pipeline (in other words, one size does not fit all). Each segment has different requirements for success with any program, and those requirements must be clear.

Even before the conclusion of this project, the Pipeline has led to changes in the way Enterprise Saskatchewan is viewing and evaluating new proposals for funding from service providers in the Province. The first change is the emphasis now being placed on being customer-driven versus solution driven. Proposed solutions are being examined for their ability to meet the identified needs of a particular market segment.

The second change has been a shift in focus from the business to the entrepreneur, which had been previously missing. If entrepreneurs are the source of economic wealth, then investments in human capital to develop a supply of such highly skilled individuals have an important and previously underutilized role to play in the economic development of the Province. The Pipeline has provided a tool by which these investments in human capital can be made and evaluated in a more systemic manner.

Address multiple levels in the system: the whole (i.e. the Province) as well as the constituent parts (i.e. geographical regions, demographic groups and market sectors) and the relationship between them

Macro-analysis of larger economic entities like states, provinces or countries, tend to hide or obscure significant differences in the smaller economic entities of which they are comprised (Warner, 2006). This often results in uniform, one-size-fits-all policies or programs that are ill-suited to the particular needs of the individual entities.

To address this problem, data were first collected on the 18 individual micro-Pipelines within the Province and then aggregated to form the macro-Pipeline for the entire Province. This ensured that the unique properties of the parts of the larger system were not lost.

The value of this approach was demonstrated at the Strategy Faire. The room for the event was organized into 19 stations – one for each of the 18 micro-pipelines and one for the Province as a whole. Maps showing the distribution of entrepreneurs and enterprises within each Pipeline were posted on the walls. As participants moved around the room, many people were visibly taken by the significant differences between each of the Pipelines, suggesting that while such differences may be readily acknowledged, recognizing their reality is another thing entirely. These maps forced participants to respond to the needs of their Pipelines in a more fine-grained manner. The fact that they did so was reflected in the customized nature of their respective recommendations (or "deals") to address the weaknesses in each of their Pipelines.

This process also more clearly highlighted points of similarity among the individual Pipelines that could benefit from a coordinated focus and economies-of-scale. Business succession, for example, proved to be an issue in all of the Pipelines. According to the Canadian Federation of Independent Business, an estimated 71% of all entrepreneurs in Canada will be looking to pass their business on to the next generation over the next 10 years (Bruce & Picard, 2005).[3] The participants in the Strategy Faire quickly realized that this issue is more properly dealt with at the provincial level (rather than launching 18 independent initiatives), and that each Pipeline should make an appropriate contribution to that effort to ensure that its specific needs are met.

Having a common map or format by which to view their marketplace of entrepreneurs and enterprises, also made the participants confront and address the specific differences as well as the similarities in their economies. Consequently, stakeholders began to formulate more customized strategies to address their unique situation. Resource limitations caused them to seek opportunities to join together and share resources. Such limitations also motivated stakeholders to specialize in meeting certain business needs and to outsource others to organizations in other parts of the Province who can deliver the solutions they need more efficiently than they could by doing it themselves (a form of functional specialization that can lead to significant increases in the system's performance).[4]

This process also encouraged the "parts" of the system – the various micro-Pipelines – to form a very different relationship to the whole, represented by the provincial Pipeline. The negotiations (among stakeholders in the individual Pipelines and between them and those responsible for the Provincial Pipeline) began to see at the appropriate roles at the different levels in the system (i.e. the whole and the parts), as well as the points of differentiation and integration. The result is a much healthier and constructive dynamic.[5]

Build support during the planning process for action by all of the stakeholders

In addition to involving as many stakeholders as possible in every stage of the process, two approaches in particular were extremely helpful in building support. First, the process of interviewing a representative sample of entrepreneurs in order to determine their placement in the Pipeline of Entrepreneur and Enterprises provided an important way for Enterprise Saskatchewan to build relationships and engage these entrepreneurs in this project.

These interviews with almost 200 entrepreneurs throughout the Province were unique in that they focused on the entrepreneurs and their experiences over the course of their lifetimes, not on their businesses. The response by entrepreneurs to these interviews was extremely positive.[6] In fact, one of the problems encountered by interviewers was keeping the session to a manageable length of time; many interviews were lasting more than 2–3 h because of how much the entrepreneurs talked. They were excited by the rare opportunity to talk about themselves and their needs. This was an excellent problem for the project to have.

A number of entrepreneurs that were interviewed expressed an interest in not only knowing what was going to be done with the information collected from them, but also in participating in the process by which the information would be used to make decisions at the provincial level about economic development investments. In fact, during this interview process, almost a dozen entrepreneurs gave their unsolicited input (which was welcomed by the interviewers) on what they thought Enterprise Saskatchewan and the Province should do to improve support for entrepreneurs. Interestingly, all of these entrepreneurs were at the Double A skill level (12 entrepreneurs out of the 19 Double A entrepreneurs interviewed or 63%). Upon reflection, this makes sense. It is at the Double A skill level that entrepreneurs broaden their scope from their immediate community or localized region to the national or international arena; change their frame of reference from their customers, employees and suppliers to the larger environment and understand the importance of linking previous silos of functional activities (marketing, finance, and operations) into an integrated process (Lichtenstein and Lyons, 2010). They are then able to bring this perspective, level of thinking and reflection to the issues of entrepreneurship as they see them in the Province. Their suggestions (such as the need to break down the silos of government as they impact on entrepreneurs and business) reflect these abilities.

This discovery suggested two criteria for selecting entrepreneurs to participate in governance activities: that they be interested in the whole community or system, not just in participating in order to achieve some outcome of value only to themselves, and that they are capable of seeing the world more broadly, instead of just in simple, instrumental and piece-meal terms (e.g. entrepreneurs need lower taxes, better employees, less regulation, etc.). While Double A entrepreneurs are not exclusive in their interest in the whole, they are more highly qualified and able to see the world in systemic or larger terms (Lichtenstein and Lyons, 2010) – something that a governance system for entrepreneurship would benefit from greatly.

The second approach that helped build stakeholder support during the planning process was the creation and use of a new role at the Strategy Faire: a Pipeline Champion. For each of the 19 Pipelines explored at this event, an internal champion (someone from Enterprise Saskatchewan or the provincial government) and an external champion (a private sector entrepreneur) who were interested in and motivated by the success of their particular Pipeline were recruited. It was the responsibility of each pair of champions to collect as much intelligence about what was happening in their Pipeline and to propose "deals" or investments that would positively impact the weaknesses in their Pipeline. In this way, a de facto public–private partnership was created, integrating the best of both perspectives. This event had the highest percentage of entrepreneurs participating of any program sponsored by Enterprise Saskatchewan (30–35%, a fact that contributed positively to its favorable dynamics.

Model the change process by intervening in the system during the planning phase

To produce systemic change, participants must be involved in the process on a physical, mental, and emotional level. The Strategy Faire in particular was designed to encourage stakeholders to act as a system and engage in systemic change, rather than merely talking about it. In the end, the Strategy Faire was less important for the content it produced (which was not insignificant) than for the process that it modeled. The event made the theory concrete and helped the participants learn by doing. As one participant in the event stated "what I liked the best was when some of the 'fake' deals (being negotiated at the Strategy Faire without real money) started to become a reality)."

Evaluation of the outcomes

This article has described the initial phase of what is expected to be a long-term, multi-level province-wide change process to establish an operating system for entrepreneurship. A classical, quantitative evaluation of outcomes is not possible at this stage.

There were several significant outcomes from the project:

- An increase in cooperation among the three divisions within Enterprise Saskatchewan, all of whom participated in this project. Having a common framework in both the Pipeline of Entrepreneurs and Enterprises and the concept of an integrated Operating System, has enabled them to look at the same object – the population of entrepreneurs – from different perspectives in a much more productive way. As one Steering Committee member stated, "colleagues from across the organization have started to look at how we all fit together as one support system."[7] According to another, "I would say this project has definitely encouraged cross-divisional dialogue between the various ES staff. It was a topic that could be applied to each division in a different way creating a common vision in moving forward with entrepreneur development in the Province."[8]

- A change in thinking about entrepreneurship. In particular, a new focus on entrepreneurs as opposed to the business and the possibilities for *both* growth and development that this entails. This change has occurred among people in several different stakeholder groups: entrepreneurs, service providers and members of Enterprise Saskatchewan. This is reflected in the comments made by these participants:
  - "The most important realization was just that economic development depends on developing people, not providing funding or other supports to businesses (although that can be a part of the solution)."
  - "I am more aware of the distinction between skill development activities – working on the entrepreneur, and business development activities – working on the business."
  - "I used to think about growth as assisting businesses but have completely changed to think about it as human capacity development and that if the entrepreneur develops their skills they take care of their business. It is a great paradigm shift."
  - "It's encouraging to know that entrepreneurs are made, not born. We can improve individual and collective well-being by developing others."
  - "The a-ha moment for me was doing the entrepreneur interviews and being able to clearly see how the skill of the entrepreneur directly affects the business they are operating. You could tell within 5 min where the entrepreneur was and what development they needed to undertake to start moving up to the next level."[9]
- The adoption of a customer-centered focus as opposed to a tool-centered (or solution-centered) approach. While currently this change is reflected mainly in the thinking of Enterprise Saskatchewan staff (who are now requiring this information when receiving funding proposals), it is expected that changes here will radiate out to other groups within the Province (who, it is hoped, will begin to provide it without solicitation).
- The development of an outcome driven discipline, as evidenced by the use of "deal sheets" and a new emphasis on financial and social return on investment criteria for funding proposals submitted to Enterprise Saskatchewan. One steering committee member reports that "when discussing or exploring new programming I am prone to use the 'deal sheet' format[10] to (1) clearly define the market need and the segment that will be serviced and (2) put numbers around the business model that will followed, regardless of how much of a guesstimate they might be."[11]
- The emergence of a systems frame or perspective for examining entrepreneurship issues. Although it is still quite early in the change process, several

individuals are beginning to use this perspective in discussions about economic development investments. One is estimate is that at as many as 33% of the 100 external stakeholders participating in the key informant interviews and the Strategy Faire are doing so. While not a large number, these individuals represent fairly significant and influential organizations. One participant argues that "the broader constituency has really started to embrace the idea. I think it hits upon something everyone has known for a long time and that is that the system is made up of disparate parts and individually we would try to create linkages for entrepreneurs but that there was limited success at working at this in isolation."[12] Another one states that "those associated with the project are speaking a new language now. It is apparent that we are looking at entrepreneurial development in a systematic way."[13]

More than 300 people have participated in this project in various ways, and as Steering Committee members indicated, the level of engagement was very high and responses positive.[14] In a province of one million people, this number is a good start, but the seeding process must continue.

Over time, the impact of this project can be measured according to:

- How many of the recommendations produced were implemented and what outcomes resulted.
- The increase in cross-functional initiatives launched within Enterprise Saskatchewan.
- The increase in initiatives that involve multiple ministries.
- The explicit use of the Pipeline to identify and describe market segments targeted for investment.
- The use of deal sheets and return-on-investment discipline.

Insights and opportunities for community development practitioners

Community development has been moving in the right direction in recent decades, with its adjusted focus from problems to assets, its commitment to human development, and its recognition of the importance of both growth and development. These are essential elements of a transformation in community quality of life. One way to support this transformation is through the creation of wealth by building business assets – entrepreneurship. Yet, for true transformation to take place a system must be created. This system must be tailored to the community in question, focus on the entrepreneur as opposed to the business, and utilize innovative tools and techniques (Lichtenstein, Lyons, & Kutzhanova, 2004). The Saskatchewan project reflects an early stage attempt to implement such a community enterprise development system.

Working at the systems level is difficult and demanding; however, success in community economic development, the ability to take the work that is currently being done in this field to the next level, requires it. The pursuit of the magic bullet – a single solution that will solve all our problems is misguided and a waste of precious resources. Instead, we must find combinations of solutions, linked together in customizable ways, to meet the unique needs of our communities and entrepreneurs.

But the desire to work at the systems level is not enough. The capacity must be there as well as tools and methods which are sophisticated enough to explicitly, honestly and directly face the complexity and multi-dimensional nature of these issues. Most analytical, as well as organizational, tools are not sufficiently deep. We as a society must discard or adapt them and find or develop new ones. Otherwise, the gulf between theory and practice in this arena will continue.

It is one thing to be able to think about these issues, and another to be able to successfully act on them in order to produce change. After reviewing the recommendations in the final report, some individuals told us that they "knew this already." However, it was clear from their comments that they did not mean that the research team simply provided them with a re-hash of their own knowledge. Rather, what they seemed to be saying is that for them, the recommendations tapped into what they knew (intuitively, perhaps not quite consciously in some cases), but did not know how to achieve. There is a vast difference between knowing *what*, and knowing *how*. It is the latter kind of knowledge researchers and practitioners need to value and cultivate.

This work requires a certain level of trust in the change agent as well as a willingness to fail in support of learning (an entrepreneurial behavior). After the Strategy Faire was over, many individuals told the research team that they did not believe it was going to work. Yet, to their credit, they were willing to take the risk to explore this territory, which proved to be very beneficial to all involved.

The Pipeline of Entrepreneurs and Enterprises and the process by which it was used in Saskatchewan give promise for its generalization to other contexts. The Pipeline demonstrated its adaptability to a variety of communities, demographic groups and industries within the Province. The process brought together a highly diverse group of stakeholders (in terms of perspectives, goals and ideologies) and facilitated their agreement on a way forward in their enterprise development activities.

Communities and practitioners considering this approach to creating an entrepreneurship system should consider the following:

(1) Identify both an internal and external change agent to facilitate the process. Success in this work requires both roles acting in combination. Either one alone will be insufficient.
(2) Create a systems frame or perspective from which to examine the issue at stake. Explore the entrepreneurship system from multiple levels.
(3) Engage in a diagnosis of the issue, before considering any solutions.
(4) Focus discussion of the impact of the current problems as well as potential solutions on the clients – the entrepreneurs.
(5) Use the Pipeline of Entrepreneurs and Enterprises to segment the market-place in a useful manner. Avoid one-size-fits-all solutions.
(6) Produce actionable recommendations and evaluate the payback, even if speculative.[15]
(7) Create a participatory process that is pragmatic, practical, and produces small, but progressive wins.

Acknowledgements

The authors thank Ciara Pierce and Steve Cardella for assistance in preparing this article.

Notes

1. This analysis of entrepreneur's statements according to their position in the Pipeline is the only way to accurately interpret such comments and determine what must be done in terms of an intervention. The need for new financing mechanisms in the lower left hand corner of the Pipeline became extremely clear, as well as the nature of the financing that was necessary. A one-size-fits-all response would not have been effective for anyone.
2. Response reported to Collaborative Strategies in a formal Evaluation of the Pipeline Analysis Project completed by Steering Committee members.
3. No such data exist at the provincial level. Having it would enable better decision-making.
4. One example of this was the existence of an organization that specialized in addressing the human resource needs of entrepreneurs and small businesses. It was the only agency in the Province that specializes in this area, and was recognized for doing a very good job. Instead of other regions attempting to start a similar organization to offer this assistance, it was strongly suggested that this organization expand to take care of the needs of entrepreneurs in other parts of the Province.
5. The succession issue is an example of this process; each region of the Province needs this kind of assistance, and yet small adaptations must be made to meet the unique requirements of their location.
6. Only a small handful of entrepreneurs were difficult to talk to and get information out of (no more than 7 out of 193); they were the exception. The individuals conducting the interviews were expecting that the difficult interviews would be the norm.
7. Ibid.
8. Ibid.
9. Ibid.
10. These are the forms used to capture the deals that were created at the Strategy Faire.
11. Ibid.
12. Ibid.
13. Ibid.
14. This can be measured specifically by the lack of political "blowback" that was expected by the project leader of Enterprise Saskatchewan. It was anticipated that many people would contact the Premier and the various offices associated with this project to complain. To their surprise, no one did so.
15. Ask yourself is the recommendation is capable of being implemented and if the description provided tells you how to do that. If not, start over again.

References

Ackoff, R.L., & Emery, F.E. (1972). *On purposeful systems*. Chicago, IL: Adline-Atherton.

Ackoff, R.L. (1981). *Creating the corporate future*. New York: John Wiley and Sons.

Arrow, K., Bolin, B., Costanza, R., Dasgupta, P., Folke, C., Holling, C.S., et al., Pimentel, D. (1995). Economic growth, carrying capacity, and the environment. *Science, 268*, 520–521.

Beer, S. (1985). *Diagnosing the system for organizations*. New York: John Wiley & Sons.

Birch, D. (1979). *The job generation process*. Cambridge, MA: MIT Program on Neighborhood and Regional Change.

Bruce, D., & Picard, D. (2005). *Succession can breed success* (pp. 3). Canada: Canadian Federation of Independent Business (CFIB) Research.

Carree, M.A., & Thurik, A.R. (2010). *The impact of entrepreneurship on economic growth*. New York: Springer Science + Business Media, LLC.

Ciegis, R., & Gineitiene, D. (2008). Participatory aspects of strategic sustainable development planning in local communities: Experience of Lithuania. *Technology & Economic Development of Economy, 14*, 107–117.

Cypher, J.M., & Dietz, J.L. (2009). *The process of economic development*. London: Routledge.

Dewar, M.E. (1998). Why state and local economic development programs cause so little economic development. *Economic Development Quarterly, 12*(1), 68–87.

Dunn, E. Jr. (1974). *Social information processing and statistical systems – change and reform*. New York: John Wiley & Sons.

Fisher, K., Geenen, J., Jurcevic, M., McClintock, K., & Davis, G. (2009). Applying asset-based community development as a strategy for CSR: A Canadian perspective on a win-win for stakeholders and SME's. *Business Ethics: A European Review, 18*(1), 66–82.

Fortunato, M.W.-P., & Alter, T.R. (2011). The individual-institutional-opportunity nexus: An integrated framework for analyzing entrepreneurship development. *Entrepreneurship Research Journal, 1*(1), Article 6.

Granovetter, M. (1985). Economic action and social structure: The problem of embeddedness. *American Journal of Sociology, 91*, 481–510.

Katsenelinboigen, A. (1984). *Some new trends in systems theory.* Seaside, CA: Intersystems Publications, 1985.

Kretzmann, J., & McKnight, J.P. (1996). Assets-based community development. *National Civic Review, 85*, 23.

Levine, R. (1997). Financial development and economic growth: Views and agenda. *Journal of Economic Literature, XXXV,* 688–726.

Lichtenstein, G.A., & Lyons, T.S. (2010). *Investing in entrepreneurs: A strategic approach for strengthening your regional and community economy.* Santa Barbara, CA: Praeger/ABC-CLIO.

Lichtenstein, G.A., & Lyons, T.S. (2006). Managing the community's pipeline of entrepreneurs and enterprises: A new way of thinking about business assets. *Economic Development Quarterly, 20,* 377–386.

Lichtenstein, G.A., Lyons, T.S., & Kutzhanova, N. (2004). Building entrepreneurial communities: The appropriate role of enterprise development activities. *Special Issue on Entrepreneurship in Community Development for the Journal of the Community Development Society, 35*(1), 5–24.

Lichtenstein, G.A., & Lyons, T.S. (2001). The entrepreneurial development system: Transforming business talent and community economies. *Economic Development Quarterly, 15*: 3–20.

Loveridge, S. (2007). Getting started in community-based entrepreneurship. In N. Walzer (Ed.), *Entrepreneurship and local economic development* (pp. 255–273). Lanham, MD: Lexington Books.

Markley, D., Macke, D., & Luther, V.B. (2005). *Energizing entrepreneurs: Charting a course for rural communities.* Lincoln, NE: RUPRI Center for Rural Entrepreneurship and Heartland Center for Leadership Development.

Phillips, R., & Pittman, R.H. (2009). *An introduction to community development.* London: Routledge.

Porter, M.E. (2000). Location, competition, and economic development: Local clusters in a global economy. *Economic Development Quarterly, 14*(1), 15–34.

Porter, M.E., & Kramer, M.R. (2011). The big idea: Creating shared value. *Harvard Business Review, 89,* 78–92.

Varol, C., Eroskum, O.Y., & Gurer, N. (2011). Local participatory mechanisms and collective actions for sustainable urban development in Turkey. *Habitat International, 35*(1), 9–16.

Wall, B. (2004). *The promise of Saskatchewan: A new vision for Saskatchewan's economy* (pp. 7).

Warner, M.E. (2006). Putting child care in the regional economy: Empirical and conceptual challenges and economic development prospects. *Community Development: Journal of the Community Development Society, 37,* 7–22.

Index